. . . stop and consider the wondrous works of God.
Job 37:14 ESV

Nonfiction Books by Amanda Dykes

A Pocketful of Wonder:
50 Hands-On Adventures for Kids to Discover God's Creation

Fiction Books by Amanda Dykes

Whose Waves These Are
Set the Stars Alight
Yours Is the Night
All the Lost Places
Born of Gilded Mountains

NOVELLAS

Up from the Sea from *Love at Last:*
Three Historical Romance Novellas of Love in Days Gone By

From Roots to Sky from *The Kissing Tree:*
Four Novellas Rooted in Timeless Love

A POCKETFUL OF WONDER

50 Hands-On Adventures for Kids to Discover God's Creation

AMANDA DYKES

BETHANY HOUSE

a division of Baker Publishing Group
Minneapolis, Minnesota

Published by Bethany House Publishers
Minneapolis, Minnesota
BethanyHouse.com

Bethany House Publishers is a division of
Baker Publishing Group, Grand Rapids, Michigan

Printed in China

Library of Congress Cataloging-in-Publication Data
Names: Dykes, Amanda, author.
Title: A Pocketful of Wonder: 50 hands-on adventures for kids to discover God's creation / Amanda Dykes.
Description: Minneapolis: Bethany House Publishers, a division of Baker Publishing Group, [2025] | Includes bibliographical references.
Identifiers: LCCN 2024022201 | ISBN 9780764242939 (cloth) | ISBN 9781493448067 (ebook)
Subjects: LCSH: Christian education—Teaching methods. | Creative activities and seat work.
Classification: LCC BV1534 .D88 2025 | DDC 268/.432—dc23/eng/20240613
LC record available at https://lccn.loc.gov/2024022201

Cover design by Jennifer Parker
Illustrations by Amanda Dykes

Published in association with Books & Such Literary Management, BooksAndSuch.com.

Baker Publishing Group publications use paper produced from sustainable forestry practices and postconsumer waste whenever possible.

25 26 27 28 29 30 31   7 6 5 4 3 2 1

For Bella, Isaiah, Jack, and Liam.

You are my greatest adventure.

May wonder strengthen your hearts for the years to come,
and draw you always to the heart of
the One who created it all . . .
and who created you.

I love you forever.

CONTENTS

ALONG THE WAY 91

SEASONS 113

DAY 145

NIGHT 153

JOURNEY'S END 163

INTRODUCTION FOR CAREGIVERS

In a land full of storybook wonder . . .

Oceans take to the sky in the form of clouds. Miraculous mid-air mountains, weighing tons and yet sheltering, not crushing us.

A molten star launches rays, sending each one off for a 93-million-mile journey, zinging past meteors, grazing stardust and frigid straits . . . then landing only minutes later in the warmth of a child's hand in a sunbeam.

And then there is the silver ruler of night. Conducting shadows, outshining distant stars, yet containing no light of its own, and pulling entire oceans in rising tides.

Flying oceans . . . zinging starlight . . . silver-pulled waves . . . this world's beauty is preposterous. Extravagant. Lavish, breathtaking, even occasionally fantastical. Yet the most astonishing thing about this world is that it is the living canvas of a Most High God who is every day painting His love for us in sweeping sunsets, in the kiss of a breeze, in a snatch of laughter, or in the dance of a tiny umbrella flung from a dandelion. These creations sing a constant song of their Creator. One who is mighty. Loving. Kind. Creative. Brilliant. Present. More faithful than the sunrise, more constant than the tide.

As we invite the children in our care to interact with God's handiwork, they will come to know Him and His love for them better and more truly while building a wonder-spotting habit that fortifies and shapes their hearts for a lifetime.

Creation is a love letter to every one of us. It "pours forth speech" (Psalm 19:2 NRSV), infusing our hearts with the courage, comfort, and hope that comes from taking the time to be filled with this thought:

If God can do this . . . He can do anything!

HOW TO USE THIS BOOK

Each page contains five elements. This simplicity is on purpose—to offer a peaceful place for you to take in wonder with the children in your care. Though geared toward adventurers ages 3–7, the engaging rhyme will interest souls even younger, and the activities and ponderings are inviting to older children too.

Flip through the pages or skim the table of contents to become acquainted with the topics. Then, when an opportune moment arises on an outing or in your day-to-day lives, return to the relevant entry and dive in. That's it! Truly.

The purpose of each entry is to broaden the moment, not crowd it. To recognize the true gift is in the moment itself, and in the turning of our hearts onto our Creator.

THE FIVE P'S: PAUSE, PONDER, PRAY, PLAY, PAIR

Pause

A poem to wrap the moment in delight-filled language, putting words to something you and your little ones see or hope to see, whether from your window or out in the park, trail, yard, or neighborhood.

Ponder

A few simple lines to foster thought and invite your child to witness the everyday miracle taking place—and then to leave plenty of room for their own observing, chattering, and noticing.

Pray

A prayer for the lasting effects of this moment to run deep.

Play

A no-prep or low-prep hands-on activity to engage your child's heart, imagination, body, and spirit.

Pair

A suggested musical piece to play as background to your activity for multisensory delight. Each piece has been selected for the way its tone echoes the theme.

Tip: Because the music and poems often have differing cadences, avoid playing the song during the poem-reading, saving it instead to enjoy afterward. A prepared playlist can be found at WonderWoodAdventures.com.

Each entry closes with a related scripture to anchor the moment in the most beautiful truth of all.

TREASURE HUNT INSIDE THE BOOK

Tucked within the full-page illustrations throughout the book are familiar friends for your child to have fun spotting: a squirrel (sometimes a few) and three dragonflies. The final illustration, *Journey's End*, contains one hidden element from each of the nine previous illustrations. Happy searching!

PERSONALIZING FOR ACCESSIBILITY, DEVELOPMENTAL SEASONS, SCHEDULES, AND MORE

Think of each entry as a *delight* list, rather than a *to-do* list. Use only what works best for you.

If part of the entry doesn't suit your needs, omit those lines and use the rest of the entry. For example, on a day that doesn't have margin for a bit of extra mess, skip the invitation to splash in a puddle.

In consideration for differing comfort levels with sensory experiences, some entries that involve more "rustic" elements (such as touching a bird's feather) offer a hands-on activity as well as a no-touch alternative.

Wonder takes many forms, and the activities offered try to remain accessible to people of all abilities. In some cases, alternate wording is provided in hopes of embracing children who are navigating life without sight, sound, or with differing physical abilities. No one knows your child better than you, and further modifications to meet their beautifully unique needs are wholeheartedly encouraged.

ADVENTURE KIT

While many activities use only the materials available on the spot (no prep required!), having the following supplies on hand in a grab-and-go adventure kit will widen your possibilities.

- Crayons
- Spiral-bound notebook of unlined paper for each child's nature journal
- Basic twine or skein of yarn
- Kid-friendly scissors inside a hard-sided container
- A roll of masking tape
- A glue stick

- Sidewalk chalk
- A set of watercolor paints and paintbrushes
- A lidded container that you can fill with water for water-color painting
- A small spray bottle for water
- A magnifying glass
- Binoculars
- Sculpting dough
- Hand-cleaning wipes or sanitizer
- Picnic blanket for on-the-go seating

Back at home, create a place to keep treasures collected on your walks. Options include:

- **Wonder Garland:** A length of twine strung across a wall, mantel, window, or elsewhere, along with small clothes-pins for pinning up pressed or dried leaves or flowers, twigs, etc.
- **Wonder Jar:** similar to the wonder garland, but simply place your gathered treasures into an oversized jar. It be-comes a centerpiece or fun conversation piece. We keep ours on a bookshelf near the children's books so that they can see and remember their outings often.
- **Flower/leaf press** (or wax paper and heavy books)
- A **portfolio** (binder, accordion file, or memory bin) to collect keepsake wonder-art.

Tip: Start your adventure kit with just a few basics. Then, as you're seeking out gifts for upcoming holidays, choose some of the bigger-ticket items to build out that adventure kit over time and help it become something that's very special. Building it like this can help your child more deeply enjoy and explore each item, as opposed to giving them the whole treasure trove at once.

THE ADVENTURE BEGINS

*A journey is waiting to lend
marvels, ideas, as friends.
Where sky is the ceiling
and you'll get the feeling
adventure is just 'round the bend.*

*We'll see many joys today,
treasures to help light the way.
These sights and this story,
these glimpses of glory
show miracles every day.*

*As you step foot outside of your door,
keep watch for surprises and more.
A bug or a cloud,
sounds quiet or loud,
and thoughts that can make our hearts soar!*

PONDER

Did you know that God knew just where you would be today? He knows what we're about to explore, and there are so many wonders to discover . . . things that when He created them, He knew you would be looking at them one day! God's Word promises He will be with us wherever we go. He'll be with us every step of the way on our adventure today!

PRAY ....

Thank you, Lord, for making this world for us to explore. Today, as we begin our adventure, please give us safety, and help us notice the things you have created: birds that fly, insects that crawl, weather in the sky, people passing by . . . you made them all, and you made us too. Thank you for your good creations, and for loving us!

PLAY ....

Favorite Things

To help foster a sense of expectancy and anticipation, here are some questions to ask as you begin your journey:

1) "What do you hope you'll see/hear/experience today?" Talk back and forth about their hopes and wishes, having fun with the conversation.

2) Tell kids to be on the lookout for a *favorite* thing they see, hear, feel, or learn. Say, "When we come back, we'll share our favorite things!" This invites adventurers to dream and hope, but also to be on the lookout for surprise experiences that they wouldn't have even known to dream of.

3) On your journey back, say, "Favorite things time!" Talk together about what they each remember and why. Ask follow-up questions, and teach them to do the same. For example, if a child says, "I liked the feather," you might follow up with a simple "That was such a fun thing to see, wasn't it? Can you tell me what you liked about it?" See more examples of Curiosity Questions in Further Resources at the end of this book.

PAIR..

Sonata No. 48 in C Major,
Hob. XVI:35: I. Allegro con brio

Joseph Haydn

⁓

*For you shall go out in joy
and be led forth in peace . . .*

ISAIAH 55:12 ESV

This poem can be used at the start of your very first adventure, or at the start of several (or all). Repetition can offer a sense of familiarity, belonging, and tradition.

SUN

PAUSE

The sunrays fill the sky so bright
They fill it up with warmth and light
I close my eyes and lift my face
and catch their falling, dashing race

A starlight blanket no one sees
It covers me in galaxies
It zinged through space and zoomed through time
to wrap me up in light sublime

It lands on earth and makes things grow
It melts the ice, sets dark aglow
It warms the air, the wind it stirs
Makes oceans dance in waves and whirrs.

PONDER

The sunlight you feel on your skin right now left the surface of the sun only a few minutes ago! It really was zooming through outer space, past meteors, planets, and stardust, before landing on you right now. Isn't it a wonder? If you're ever feeling down, find a patch of sunlight to sit in and think to yourself, *If God can zoom light from a star all the way here—all the way to me, right in this moment—to keep me warm and give me light . . . then He can do anything!*

PRAY

Lord, when you created the world, the very first words you spoke were "Let there be light" (Genesis 1:3 NIV). Light is important to you, and you gave it to us to do wonderful things with. When we do things in the light, we pray they will help others and give you honor. Show us how you would like us to use the light today . . . and thank you, Lord, for the gift of light!

PLAY

Sunlight Welcome Party

To help kids grasp both the closeness and the distance of the source of our light, create an impromptu "welcome party" for those sunrays. Bring out pots and pans and wooden spoons, kazoos, or any other fun noisemakers. Set the timer for eight minutes and twenty seconds. Tell kids that's how long it takes for rays of light to travel from the sun, all the way to us. Talk together about some of the things between us and the sun—places so cold they near absolute zero, where all motion stops. Meteors, planets, darkness—the rays of light are passing right through all of it.

Start the timer together and do something related to fill the time—perhaps coloring a "Welcome, Sunrays!" sign, or cutting up bits of confetti from construction paper. When the timer goes off, kids erupt into cheers, banging pots and pans, tossing confetti, holding up their signs. You can talk about how the sunlight isn't alive and can't understand what we're doing, but we can still be excited to welcome a creation of God, which He made to miraculously travel those outer-space wilds, just to get to us and light up our lives, along with giving us warmth, helping plants grow, and nourishing our bodies (vitamin D). We can give Him thanks for providing for us in such a mighty, miraculous way. Let kids play, jumping up in sun spots, reveling in the fact that something that moments ago was grazing meteors and stardust is now landing right on them.

PAIR..

"Polka Italienne"

Sergei Rachmaninoff

~

[Give thanks] to him who made the great lights,
for his steadfast love endures forever;
the sun to rule over the day . . .

PSALM 136:7–8 ESV

*This poem is written in **iambic tetrameter**.*

To try this fun meter in a poem of your own,
use this rhythm and length for each line:

ba-DUM ba-DUM ba-DUM ba-DUM

PAUSE..

Here it comes
Drumming drums
On the walls of every building
Like the crash-and-splash-and-thrash
Of ocean waves (*whoosh, whoosh*)

It's the wind!
Mighty gust
Somersaulting over mountains
With a flurry-scurry-hurry
Churning land (*swoosh, swoosh*)

Twirling and swirling,
Furling, unfurling
Going-blowing-slowing
Then it rests
(*shhh . . .*)

Now it's up!
It comes back!
Like a roundabout riddle
It's a prance-a-dance-a-chance
For things to fly (*oh my . . .*)

Here's a howl
Does it scowl?
It's a blast-a-blow-a-beast
Or perhaps a laughing feast—
Confetti toss (*look out!*)

Whistling and rustling,
Bristling and bustling

Building-growing-stowing
Then it sighs
(*ah . . .*)

Now a breeze
Moves with ease
With a gallop and a skip
And a clip-a-dip-a-trip
Still far to go (*tallyho . . .*)

Then it taps
Blows in gaps
Tosses diamonds through the sky
With a huff-a-puff-a-scuff
Unwrapping cold (*brrr . . .*)

And the wind
That wild creature
Settles down, a quiet feature
When it **whispers**- whispers- whispers
Gentle things (*hush, hush . . .*)

PONDER...

It's fun to imagine that the wind rippling through your hair has also swooped its way over rooftops, mountains, treetops and more— and is going other places now too. The wind can feel so mighty! But just by standing there, being you, standing firm, you change the course of the wind. God uses you to make a mighty difference, even in the swirl of mighty things!

PRAY ....

God, even though the wind is invisible, it changes the earth in all sorts of ways. Thank you that you are like this too: You can move mountains, even though we don't see you. Please help our faith and trust in you to grow . . . and thank you for the wind!

PLAY ....

Fly a Kite

Bring a kite to an open-sky area and have some fun with wind-play! Help your kids feel personally connected to the activity by

- Inviting them to help assemble the kite. Coach them through age-appropriate steps.
- Giving them permanent markers to draw a picture of themselves, and/or write their name on the kite. For younger children, trace the outline of their hand on the kite. Tell them, "This means your name [or picture] will be in the air soon, way up there! How high do you think 'you' will go?"
- Helping them fly the kite. Depending on the wind conditions and how hard it is to get the kite up, you can get it airborne and then hand it off to them, standing by to help tug and guide the kite as needed.

PAIR...

Maskarad (Masquerade): I. Waltz

Aram Khachaturian

⁓

For behold, he who forms the mountains and creates the wind . . .
and treads on the heights of the earth—
the LORD, the God of hosts, is his name!

AMOS 4:13 ESV

CLOUDS

PAUSE..

Brontosaurus billowing
Pigs and piglets pillowing
Cloud parade—
Cloud charade!
Floating treetops willowing

Fluffy stepping stones up there
Journey through the sky
Sunbeams playing leapfrog
Giants passing by!

Rounding rises bounding
Misty mountains mounding
Lovelies loft,
Wind-scapes waft,
Cats in capes confounding

Shifting shadows weave up there
into tucks of light
Shuffling with the sunset
Painting all things bright

Oceans rearranging
Colors so engaging
Sky's a stage
For any age—
Canvas ever-changing

PONDER

Clouds are made of tiny little bits of water, like the steam that comes out of a tea kettle, floating up into the air. Even though that tea kettle was heavy when you filled it up in the sink, some of that same heavy water is now flying, as if were as light as air!

We can think of clouds as flying water too. There's so much water up there, you might even call it a flying ocean. Even though all that water is heavy, when it's up there in those little bits that make up clouds, we are safe. In fact, sometimes those clouds—those flying oceans—even help protect us from things like sunburn.

Have you ever seen how light bounces and slides along the surface of a creek as the water moves? Look at those clouds and just think: those clouds are made of water too. Can you imagine everything that sunlight is doing up there on top of those clouds right now? Sliding this way and that, bouncing off of it and reflecting onto hills and trees and mountains, creating shadows way down here. It must be fun to imagine being a sunbeam on a cloud!

PRAY

God, help us to notice the miracles of clouds. Remind us to see the way they show us you are mighty and good, creative and kind.

PLAY

Lay on some soft grass or your picnic blanket and watch the clouds for a while. Point out things you see, how things move, and marvel that the scene playing out before you is an interplay of wind, light, and flying sea . . . and it's a once-in-a-lifetime show! No one will ever see this exact display again.

Cloud Games

- **Scavenger Hunt:** Say, "Let's see who can spot a cloud or patch of blue sky that looks like an animal!" *or* "Can anyone see a cloud that's near a tree? How about a cloud that's moving?"
- **Charades:** Invite children to pick a creature, perhaps one they've spotted in the clouds, and to act it out, letting you guess what it is.

PAIR...

Paquita: Variation 5. Allegro non troppo (by Cherepnin)

Léon Fyodorovich Minkus

⁓

He wraps up the waters in his clouds,
yet the clouds do not burst under their weight.

JOB 26:8 NIV

THUNDER

If a noise could tumble,
Pick you up and make you fly
It would be the thunder
Rolling through the sky

It would vault you over mountains
It would loft you over streams
It would bounce you in its ripples
Like the clouds could give you wings

Then you'd ride that rumble,
And slide down its rising song
You might feel its mighty tremble
Humming stormily along

You could look down at the treetops,
You could leap on mountaintops
You could land upon the rooftops
Flying up to play hopscotch

So as you hear that thunder
In the safety of your home
Close your eyes and imagine
An adventure of your own.

PONDER

When we're safe and warm inside during a thunderstorm, it's fun to imagine what it would be like to ride that rumbling sound. Don't worry; thunder doesn't *really* pick us up and carry us away. But it is pretty amazing that something from way up in the sky could rumble through the air, sometimes so loud that we can feel it! It comes after a bolt of lightning makes the bits of air around it *so* very hot that those air particles dance around like crazy, bumping into each other and making all that noise. It's the sky's way of singing a song as a result of bright light!

PRAY

God, the thunder feels so mighty . . . but you are mightier still! Your Word tells us that you are "mightier than the thunder of the great waters"—and that includes the bits of water and ice in the clouds, moving around and making all that noise. Thank you that thunder can remind us of how powerful you are, and how that power is always carried in your love.

PLAY

Thunder Hopscotch

Using masking tape that can be easily peeled up later, create a hopscotch course on a floor inside. When the thunder starts, kids hop and see how far they can get before the thunder stops, leaving a marker on the farthest square they reached. They can try to beat that on the next go-round.

Thunder Paint

Using watercolors, invite kids to paint what they hear or see. For an extra dose of whimsical fun, put a cup outside to catch rainwater, and then let them use the rainwater to paint their scene. Marvel together in the wonder of using water that minutes ago was held above you in clouds miles up in the air! Talk together about how the raindrops could have passed right through the source of the thunder . . . and now they're holding that water in their hands, creating something beautiful.

PAIR..

For something intense to match the thunder:

Palladio: I. Allegretto

Karl Jenkins

For something to temper the thunder with comfort:

Cello Sonata No. 3 in A major, Op. 69:
III. Adagio cantabile

Ludwig Van Beethoven

⁓

Mightier than the thunder of the great waters,
mightier than the breakers of the sea—
the Lord on high is mighty.

Psalm 93:4 niv

LIGHTNING

PAUSE

Zap . . .

   Zing!

      Split-the-sky—

Fling!

Bright . . .

   Slash!

      Blink-your-eyes—

Flash!

Quick . . .

   Bolt!

      Map-the-clouds—

Jolt!

PONDER

Did you know that lightning is so powerful, it heats up the air around it to be five times hotter than the surface of the sun? That means that for a flash of a moment, parts of the earth are hotter than the star that heats us. How amazing! Lightning can be startling, but it also helps the earth by putting something called nitrogen into the soil that can help things grow, like the fruit we eat!

In the same way, sometimes we might feel startled by things that happen to us, but challenges can help us grow strong too.

PRAY

Lord, you have created this world so that it's full of miracles. A flash of light falling to earth in the middle of the storm helps things grow . . . which helps us grow too? That's a miracle! Thank you for the way you provide good things for us. Help us to be courageous when things are scary or hard, to remember that you use those things to help us grow too . . . and that you are always, always with us! You are the light of the world, and you shine inside us even brighter than lightning.

PLAY

Lightning Race

On the floor, let kids arrange some yarn, spare sheets, or blankets in the shape of lightning. Then they can run alongside their creations to "map" the lightning with their feet. For deeper interaction with the storm, anyone can shout out, "Lightning!" when they see a flash of lightning outside, and kids can jump as high as they can, hands in the air, and then continue their race.

Lightning Sculpt

For a quieter activity, bring out the sculpting dough and invite kids to sculpt clouds, lightning bolts, and raindrops, laying them out on the surface in a storm design. Or, they could squish/roll their dough into a flat "canvas" and carve a storm scene into it using a plastic knife or other tool.

PAIR ....

For something striking to match the lightning:

Symphony No. 5 in C Minor, Op. 67: I. Allegro con brio

Ludwig Van Beethoven

For something less ominous but still jaunty and "zig-zaggy,"
for those who could use something lighter in the middle of a storm:

"Wedding Day at Troldhaugen"

Edvard Grieg

~

He causes the clouds to rise over the whole earth.
He sends the lightning with the rain
and releases the wind from his storehouses.

PSALM 135:7 NLT

Some lightning flashes within its own cloud,
Some goes from cloud to earth,
and some jumps from cloud to cloud!

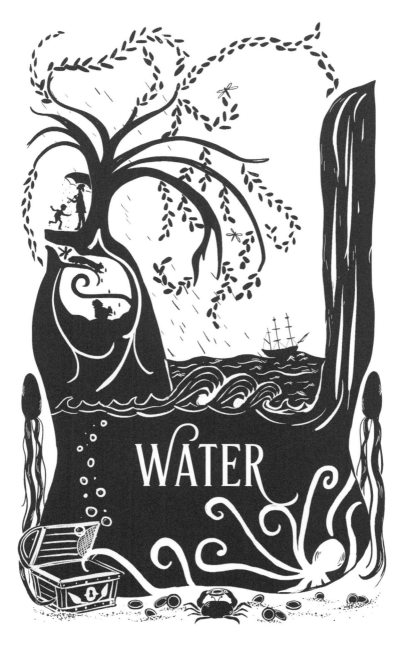

WATER

WATER

Splashing, sloshing,
Running, galoshing,
Water likes to flow
From mist rising high
To clouds in the sky
And raindrops falling low

A pond or a puddle,
A lake or a bubble
It's wonderful to know
This water right here
wasn't always right here—
God made it long ago!

PONDER

Did you know that water likes to take trips? It rises up sometimes, it falls down sometimes, it travels all over in rivers and streams. So that raindrop you just caught traveled to you from places and times far away! Maybe it carried a ship on the ocean, once upon a time. Maybe a whole family of fish wiggled through it in the sea. Maybe it was even right there when God first created water!

PRAY

God, thank you for water! Thank you for how it helps us in so many ways. What a beautiful story you tell through the many journeys that water takes. It shows us how creative and exciting you are!

PLAY ....

Vanishing Paint

If possible, using your adventure kit's lidded container, gather a bit of water from the feature you're watching (puddle, creek, pond, lake, fountain, sprinkler, etc.). Using the paintbrushes from your watercolor kit, let kids use the gathered water—without paint—to create a "disappearing painting" on a rock, sidewalk, or other surface. Alternately, paint using the watercolors and paper in your kit, along with the water you've gathered. Talk together with fun conversation starters like

I love what you're painting. Can you tell me about it?

I see you're using the color _____ . What a great choice. Look around. Do you see that color in other things nearby?

What are some fun places this water might have been before in its travels? Do you think fish ever swam through it in an ocean? Do you think it ever flew in the sky as part of a cloud?

PAIR..

Gli uccelli (The Birds), P. 154: V. "Il cucu": Allegro

Ottorino Respighi

〜

When you pass through the waters, I will be with you . . .

Isaiah 43:2 esv

TIDE

A
hidden world
waits beneath
these salty ocean waves
A universe
of water over
secret pools and caves

Two
times a day
the water climbs, it reaches up so high
Two times a day, it rolls on back
retreating like
a sigh

Pulled
back like a
curtain in a marvelous reveal,
it leaves behind a fortune of these
treasures
unconcealed:

Shells
on boulders,
seaweed twisting,
finned things swim about;
Shells
are moving,
starfish stretching,
urchins crawling out

Then up
it comes, the climbing sea,
to hide this world once more:
A bubbling swishing hush
beneath waves
reach-
-ing for the
shore.

PONDER...

At this very moment, somewhere in the world, the ocean is creeping up into high tide or crawling out in low tide. It does this twice a day . . . but why? Believe it or not, it has to do with the moon, which pulls on the earth with a mighty force called gravity, a little bit like how a magnet pulls metal toward it.

So when you see that moon up in the sky, think of the crashing ocean out there somewhere, reaching for it. It sounds like something enchanted—but it's God's beautiful design.

PRAY..

Lord, you are more faithful than the tides. You created them! No one can stop them, and no one can block you from doing exactly what you would like to do in our lives. Thank you for your strength and faithfulness.

PLAY..

Walking on the Water's Home

After checking tide charts, weather, and other conditions to ensure safety, visit a shore known for tide pools at low tide to see what you can spot. Pull out the magnifying glass and notice everything from barnacles to moving creatures, taking care with any that may be toxic. On the squishy tidal flats, invite kids to make a design on the freshly revealed earth with footprints or stick-drawn lines. Marvel together that just a few hours ago, this entire place was covered in ocean . . . and in just a few hours more, the water will climb over their very footprints again.

Paint the Ocean

If you're not close enough to explore tidal flats or pools at the ocean, pull out the watercolors and invite your kids to paint the sea, filling it with creatures imaginary or real. For inspiration, peruse pictures together in books or watch tide pool exploration videos online.

PAIR..

"Sea Songs"

Ralph Vaughan Williams

Notice the lively notes ascending and descending by turns. How does that resemble the tide?

⌣

Look at the ocean, so big and wide!
It is filled with more creatures than people can count.
It is filled with living things, from the largest to the smallest.

PSALM 104:25 NIRV

Turn the poem sideways. Do the jagged lines look like waves?

PUDDLE

Toss in a stick and
Watch the ripples grow
Toss in a pebble,
It sinks down below

Twirl in a leaf
See it float and go
Blow across the water
Tiny waves show!

Jump big, jump small,
Jump fast or slow
Jump in if you dare
And feel your smile glow!

PONDER

At first, a puddle might seem like just a murky spot of muddy old water that's in the way. But when you take the time to explore it and play in it, it becomes a whole world of joy! So many places and moments in our lives can be like that. They might seem plain or boring at first, but when we pay close attention . . . something wonderful awaits!

PRAY

God, thank you for making puddles. For the way earth catches water and makes a whole new world right here in front of us. Help us remember that just like a ripple that travels far across the puddle, the things we do and say can make a big difference in the world around us.

PLAY

Puddle Voyage

Have children gather objects found nearby, then act out the actions of the poem while reading it aloud a second time.

Or help your child imagine that the leaf, feather, or other light-weight object they've set afloat is a ship. See if they can help it cross the puddle by blowing on it, aiding it with a long stick, splashing with their feet, or tossing heavier objects (like small rocks or pine-cones) to create ripples. Make guesses about where the leaf-ship will land. Name the ship and the tiny "beaches" on the outskirts of the puddle, whether it's surrounded by dirt, pavement, asphalt, or grass.

As long as their interest lasts, have fun creating this miniature water world together. Observe together what sinks and what floats, and invite them to explore why that is. Once home, make a map of your "puddle lake" together as a keepsake.

PAIR

"The Eightsome Reel"

Scottish Traditional

⌒

For I will pour water on the thirsty land,
and streams on the dry ground . . .

Isaiah 44:3 NIV

RAIN

PAUSE

Bare feet,
Palms up,
Catching sky in hand

Something special
In the air
Feel the world expand

Streams on sidewalks
Lakes on streets
A water world in motion

At the window
Tracing paths
Mapping raindrop oceans

Crowning treetops
Beading grass
Sculpting earth and sand

Making music
Drip-drip-drip
Striking up the band

Cozy inside,
Outside wild
A rumble tumbles loud

Skin prickles
Branches bounce
Down has come the cloud

Run, dance,
Jump, play
Slosh or see or stand

Everything
Is clean and new
Here where sky meets land

PONDER

What are some of your favorite things you've seen rain do today? (Splash, form little streams, lift things to float, slide down leaves, etc.) It really is wonderful, isn't it? It turns the whole world into a shining place for a little while. Did you know that the rain does *even more* than what we can see? It does invisible things too: It seeps into the earth, and helps things grow deep down in the dark.

Can you imagine? Clouds giving up their water, sending it on a journey all the way from high in the sky to deep down below—and then after that, those things grow and bring new life—even things we can eat, like apples and carrots! When you think of it like this, even something ordinary like eating becomes extraordinary! We can enjoy a delicious snack all because God designed clouds to pour down their rain in a shimmering dance to help things grow.

PRAY

God, what an amazing thing that you release water from the sky and use it to drench the earth. It waters the soil and helps food grow; it waters our hearts and helps hope grow. You create masterpieces everywhere—even in rainstorms! Thank you for the joy of rain. When skies are gray, help us remember to watch for new life and growth that happens.

PLAY ....

Rain Art (Outside)

If light to moderate rain is in the forecast, invite children ahead of time to create large colorful chalk creations on the sidewalk, porch, driveway, or anywhere that will be exposed to the rain. Concentrated "blobs" or shapes of filled-in color will give the best results. Wait for the storm to come and work its magic—it should wet and mingle the colors, bringing unexpected touches to the art.

If you're experiencing heavier rain that could wash the chalk away entirely, try a more controlled version of rain art. Using chalk or washable markers, have children fill a heavy piece of paper with concentrated shapes, blobs, concentric rings, or stripes of color. Set the paper outside for a shorter time in the rain and see what the water does to it. Use a container, such as a baking sheet, to set the paper in if you're concerned about the colors seeping onto the pavement beneath.

Raindrop Races (Inside)

As depicted in the poem, map the raindrops at a window! While cozy inside or in the car, show children how to trace the path of raindrops with their finger. They can race either against you, a sibling, a friend, or themselves if they choose two raindrops at once to see which raindrop reaches the bottom of the window first.

PAIR...

Prelude, Op. 28, No. 15 (the "Raindrop" Prelude)

Frédéric Chopin

⁓

For He draws up drops of water,
Which distill as rain from the mist,
Which the clouds drop down
And pour abundantly on man.

JOB 36:27–28 NKJV

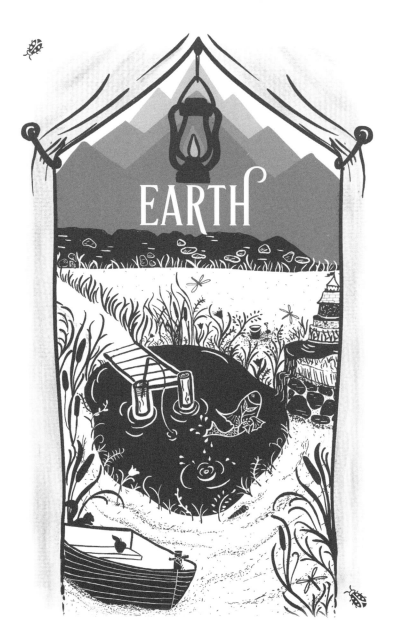

EARTH

FOOTPRINTS

PAUSE..

First the heel
Then the toe
Over, again, and off you go!

Soft footfalls,
Or hard ones too
Footprints are an echo of you.

Splash a puddle
On sidewalks
Jump where it's dry and see those spots!

Chase and journey
Caught in time,
Trace where you've been as paths unwind

Shape in earth,
Or vanishing wet,
That's where you've been . . . where to next?

PONDER..

Footprints are like a work of art, showing where you've been. Have you ever thought of all the people who have walked here before? It could be a friend . . . a brother or sister . . . someone you'll never meet but who has the same favorite color as you . . . or even someone who lived and walked here a hundred years ago! Footprints are special because they show us that we get to change the world—even the shape of it, just a little—just by being who God made you.

PRAY

Jesus, thank you that you walked this earth too. You understand where we are, where we've been, and where we'll go . . . and you give us wisdom and instruction to know which way to turn next. We pray that we will make decisions in our lives for our feet to take us places where we will serve you, know you, and help others.

PLAY

Footprint Follow

Find a place outside where you can see footprints (pavement with a sprinkler nearby, dirt/mud, or snow). Designate a "Footprint Artist." This person gets to go first, creating a design or path for others to follow. They might zig-zag, lay a path in a spiral, or make a design that creates a large picture. Everyone else in the group follows, looking for their footprints and placing their own feet in (or near) them. Take turns being the Footprint Artist until everyone has had a chance.

PAIR

"Marcha Radetzky," Op. 228

Johann Strauss I

⁓

Direct my footsteps according to your word;
let no sin rule over me.

PSALM 119:133 NIV

BEACHES

PAUSE

Land of castles
Land of clams
Land of swishing, sloshing sand
Swimming, sifting, silting free
Land that's lake or pond or sea

Sea of people
Sea of shells,
Sea of pebbles, fables, swells
Mixing, mingling, merrily
Sea where water lands

PONDER

Sometimes it appears as if the water is decorating the beach. Ribbons of seaweed strung this way and that, shells strewn about like jewels, puddles catching sunlight and glinting like diamonds. It's fun to think of the coast playing dress-up, but the truth is even more amazing: God is dressing it up for us!

PRAY

What an amazing thing, God, to watch water and land mix together, here on the shore of the [sea, river, lake, creek, etc.] Some of these waves may have started thousands and thousands of miles away, from wind or storms . . . and here it is, crashing right by our feet. It reminds us that you have created amazing possibilities . . . and that your Word says you are mightier than all that we see. You created it! Thank you for being so strong and near to us.

PLAY

Sand Drawing

Find a patch of dry sand. Dig a small hole to find the damp sand beneath. Retrieve it by the fistful, and use your fist to release it in a steady stream, moving your hand around, using the wet sand you're releasing to create designs, drawings, letters, or words on the canvas of dry sand.

You can also reverse the process. Scrape away the top layer of sand to create a canvas of dark, wet sand. Use the pile of dry/lighter sand to "drizzle" your designs on the ground.

Free play in the sand is a favorite too: making sandcastles, moats, tunnels, etc.

PAIR

Three écossaises, Op. 72 No. 3

Frédéric Chopin

Mightier than the thunders of many waters,
mightier than the waves of the sea,
the LORD on high is mighty!

PSALM 93:4 ESV

ROCKS

PAUSE..

Castles climbing up and up
Gray walls gather round
Stepping stones where we can walk
Cobbled streets on ground

Skip a rock on water,
Watch it sink below
Piece it like a puzzle
Some rocks even glow!

Breaking loose from mountains,
Crashing down the slopes
Pick them up and build them up
In pathways, homes, and hopes

Great big boulders you can climb
Tiny grains of sand
Mountains, pebbles, rocks, and stones,
Strength inside your hand

Hold one up to sunshine
Watch it catch the light
Formed within the darkness,
Now it's glinting bright

Blue of bluest sapphire
Green of emerald
Ruby red afire
Opal holds a world

Every rock's a journey,
a story to be told
Wonder in a piece of earth,
New from something old.

PONDER..

Whew, rocks can be so heavy! Sometimes they're rough and have sharp edges too. But over time, forces like wind, water, and other sand or rocks can rub off some of those rough and sharp places, carrying little, tiny bits of the rock to faraway places and leaving the rock a little smoother.

Can you find a rock to pick up? Now, just imagine. Tiny pieces of this rock could be far across the world or in a faraway sea by now, carried there by the wind or the water. God makes rocks strong, but also continues to shape them . . . a lot like what He does for us!

PRAY ....

Lord, thank you for the gift of rocks. You gave them to us to make shelters, roads, pathways, and more! You tell us that you are our Rock, our strength, our refuge—which means you are our safe place. Thank you for being our safe place, and for being so strong. Amen.

PLAY ....

Rock Architect

After gathering rocks at a field, forest, or park, encourage kids to build something: a lined pathway from one tree to another, a picture or design in the ground created by laying rocks in lines, an assortment by color, or even a small stone wall. Read *Roxaboxen* by Alice McLerran and Barbara Cooney and create your own rock-lined village. Search "pebble art" online for more ideas and inspiration.

Paint Rocks

Using kid-friendly acrylic paints, invite kids to paint colorful designs, scenes, faces, or animals on the rocks. Keep them for yourself or leave them along trails for others to find and delight in.

For a variation of this, find twenty-four flat-ish, round-ish small stones. Paint twelve in one design (such as ladybugs) and twelve in another (such as bumblebees) . . . and now you have a set of checkers! Draw a checkerboard in the sand or use a premade one to play.

PAIR..

Le Carnaval des Animaux: XII. "Fossiles"

Camille Saint-Saëns

⁓

Truly he is my rock and my salvation;
he is my fortress, I will not be shaken.

PSALM 62:6 NIV

Did you know there's a rock cycle, just like there's a water cycle? Search out books or online videos about it . . . you'll be amazed!

MUD

PAUSE..

Squish!
Make a mess
Dress the earth in your creations
Make a hill, a room, a nation
Out of dirt.

—

Squash!
Water slosh
Mix it up so you can smooth it,
Build it up so you can move it,
Start again.

—

Splat!
Pitter-Pat
Making footprints into fountains
Carving rivers into mountains,
Canyons too.

—

Drip!
Move your grip
Change the world right here, right now
And if you're wondering, wondering how—
You just did!

PONDER...

Mud can seem very ordinary—it's just dirt and water, after all. But when you stop to think of how old this dirt is, the places it's been, and the water it mixes with, the places *it's* been, and how when they mix, you can make almost anything . . . mud is a miracle! It shows us how when we take care of the things right in front of us, we can change the world in such a wonderful way. Turning simple mud into a castle? That's pretty amazing.

PRAY ....

God, thank you that you made mud. Right in the very first sentence of your Word, you tell us you created the earth—and it's so beautiful that the first sentence of your great, big story can teach us so much. You even used mud as you healed someone who was blind (John 9)! Thank you that mud can help us see amazing things too, just by playing with it.

PLAY ....

Mud Volcano (higher mess)

Mound mud into a volcano shape, hollowing out a downward tunnel from the top. Fill it with baking soda, then pour vinegar over the top to watch the "eruption"! Let kids have fun examining the "craters" made in the dirt when the fizz settles down. They may even spot shapes in them or play connect-the-dots with them, using a twig.

Mud Bricks (higher mess)

Using a rectangular container, mix mud and bake in sun. Let kids experience the unique joy of a long-term project that offers the chance to grow patience, vision, imagination, and perseverance as they create more bricks over time to build up their creation.

Mud City (higher mess)

Build a network of canals, rivers, waterfalls, pools, buildings/ rooms, etc.—and watch your mud universe grow, along with your child's expanding imagination!

Mud Impressions (lower mess)

Carefully lay leaves and twigs into mud in interesting designs, then pull the leaves off and admire the impressions made. Leave the "mud art" there to grace the day of other visitors. Or use a stick or twig to make drawings in the mud. Alternatively, do this activity in sculpting dough instead of mud.

PAIR..

"Dance of the Hours" from *La Gioconda*

Amilcare Ponchielli

(Especially starting at the two-minute mark)

⁓

In the beginning, God created
the heavens and the earth.

GENESIS 1:1 ESV

TWIG TUMBLE

PAUSE

*Up from the
ground it
goes*

*Curling a-
round it
blows*

*Air is a
whirlpool*

*Sky is a
twirl-school*

*Stirring the
dust, it
grows*

*Lassoing
leaves it
churns*

*Tasseling
twigs it
turns*

*Breeze
an invitation*

*to
slumbering creation*

*Summoning
grass and
ferns*

*Down to the
ground it
drops*

*Dancing in
starts and
stops*

*Then a
small kick-up*

*Leaping
like a hiccup*

*Weaving into
dips and
hops*

PONDER

Have you ever seen a rock in the middle of a stream? The water splits and rushes around it, then meets back together on the other side, sometimes spinning into little swirls when it does.

Did you know the wind does this too? When it has to split around something in its path, like a house or a car or a tree, it claps back together on the other side, colliding into little spins of air. As it spins, it picks up bits of dust, leaves, and grasses, making it look like a leaf merry-go-round!

It can remind us that even when something interrupts our plans, we might feel frustrated at first . . . but a lot of times, something exciting and beautiful happens as a result, just like those leaf dances.

PRAY

Lord, you are always at work! You even use invisible things like wind to set your creation to dancing. Thank you for weaving so much beauty and meaning into this world, all out of love for us.

PLAY

Leaf Tornado Collage

After watching this circular dance of the leaves, guide children in gathering bits of debris from its path, or from the place it has settled down.

Let them lay their collection on the ground, in essence leaving behind an illustration of the twig tumble. Or do the same thing, but in their nature journal rather than on the ground, taping or gluing bits of leaves, twigs, and grasses from the actual "tornado" onto their page in a tornado-like design of their making.

Lead them into wonder over the fact that they've just created art, using something that only moments ago was dancing in the air before their very eyes! Now, whenever they look at their illustration, they'll see a beautiful memory captured in time.

PAIR..

"Flight of the Bumblebee"

Nikolai Rimsky-Korsakov

～

He makes winds his messengers . . .

PSALM 104:4 NIV

When wind splits to move around something, that's called **wind shearing***.*

Afterward, when it spins and picks up little circular tumbles of leaves, twigs, and dust, those are called **wind eddies***.*

Can you think of a fun name of your own for these? Perhaps a "leaf dance" or a "twig tornado"?

WILD
THINGS

SPIDER'S WEB

PAUSE...

Clever creeping climber,
Up and up you go
Swift and soft rope-shiner
Putting on a show

Mid-air masquerader
Swing your silk trapeze
Empty-space invader
Wingless flight with ease

Weaving-building-twirling-gilding-catching-starlight-beams
Working-striving-resting-thriving-making-things-of-dreams

Silent silken spinner
Painting an array
Masterpiece beginner
Making all the day

Quiet shadow-taker
Small and quick you are
Silent music-maker
Strings like a guitar

Prancing-moving-skipping-proving-hiding-what-seems-clear
Shifting-catching-drifting-thatching-now-the-lines-appear

Tiptoe tightrope walker,
Dancing with no floor
Spindly high tree-topper
Home without a door

Make a thing of beauty
Whether someone knows
Do your spider duty
Set the air aglow

Rushing-dashing-brushing-smashing-now-your-web's-complete
Falling-tumbling-spinning-spindling-landing-on-your-feet

PONDER

Not all spiders are the type that make big round webs with carefully measured matching sections. But some do, and they're called "orb weavers." Did you know that to build something so beautiful, they first begin with a big, knotted mess in the middle? It gives them a strong place to start from. Once they've built the rest of their beautiful web, they return to the messy center . . . and eat it! Then, they replace it with the finishing touches that look nice and neat. They create these beautiful webs because it's what they were made to do, whether or not anyone is watching.

We can learn a lot from spiders, can't we? Don't worry if things you try seem like a mess sometimes—the mess is an important part! And we can do things well and with joy, no matter who is or isn't watching.

PRAY

Lord, thank you that right now, there are spiders creating silent works of art all over the world. Even when no one is watching, we can do beautiful and good things. Help us to work like that, with a full heart!

PLAY ....

Woven Color-Web

Supplies

- 2–3 medium-sized twigs, popsicle sticks, or dowels
- Yarn or twine in the color(s) of your choice, or a multi-colored yarn
- Hot glue and hot glue gun (optional)

Steps

1) Cross the sticks in the middle to create a ✳ shape (if using 3 twigs) or a ✚ shape (if using two, easier for younger kids/smaller hands). Optional: Adult hot glue sticks together at center intersection
2) Start wrapping yarn around the middle in all directions until sticks feel stationary and firm.
3) Begin "weaving" the string—wrapping it around each stick once, then moving it to the next stick and repeating, around and around the radiating form until much of the stick-structure is covered in yarn, and the space between is now filled with a colorful web of string.

PAIR ....

"Pizzicato Polka"

Johann Strauss II

~

Work at everything you do with all your heart. Work as if you were working for the Lord, not for human masters.

COLOSSIANS 3:23 NIRV

*The part of a spider that makes silk is called a **spinneret**!*

PAUSE

Come over and stoop down so low
It's here that you'll see kingdoms grow
With castles of sand
Small workers so grand
A city of tunnels below

For here in this world in between
With workers and soldiers and queen
Moving mountains complete
Right under our feet
Tiny giants of strength make a scene!

They scurry and scuttle and flee
They flurry and funnel and see
Small bits at a time
Build a kingdom so fine
Each doing their part busily.

PONDER

See that tiny ant hole? Behind that small opening in the earth, there are thousands of ants digging tunnels, and tunnels, and more tunnels. . . sometimes for miles! Ants are so small, but they can carry up to fifty times their own weight. That would be like if you could pick up a horse and scurry around with it! Please don't try to pick up a horse—but that gives you an idea of how strong these tiny ants are. Just think, every time you pass an anthill, a whole kingdom of tunnels is being made where we can't even see it. And how do they do it? One small grain of sand at a time. Sometimes, great big things happen by tiny things being done faithfully, over and over.

PRAY ....

God, your Word tells us to watch the ant and learn from it. Thank you for giving us an example of a creature that does its work, helps its friends, and builds big things by doing small things faithfully. Please help us see today how we can do small things with joy too.

PLAY ....

Mock Ant Maze

In an area clear of ants or any danger of being bitten, invite each child to trace their own mazelike path in the ground using fingers or sticks. If you wish, do an internet search for "cross-section of an ant hill" and show your kids. Or let them be guided solely by imagination. Next, have them choose a found object (twig, leaf, rock), and move it through the maze, imagining it's an ant traveling through its tunnels. For a twist on the activity, deposit a pile of pebbles to transport at the end of each maze. Whenever the child reaches the end of their maze, they retrieve a pebble, move with the "ant" back through the maze with the pebble, deposit it at the other end of the maze, and repeat until the pebble pile has been entirely transported. Talk about how this is a little bit like what the ants are doing right this very moment!

PAIR ....

Zapateado (Spanish Dance No. 6, Op. 23, No. 2)

Pablo de Sarasate

‿

. . . consider [the ant's] ways, and be wise.

PROVERBS 6:6 ESV

*The rollicking type of poem used above is called a **limerick**. To create one together, use this structure:*

Line 1: 7–10 syllables, ends in rhyme A
Line 2: 7–10 syllables, ends in rhyme A
Line 3: 5–7 syllables, ends in rhyme B
Line 4: 5–7 syllables, ends in rhyme B
Line 5: 7–10 syllables, ends in rhyme A

CREATURE TRACKS

PAUSE...

Memory keeper
Etched in sand
Footfalls frozen
Held in land

Creatures walked here,
Jumped or crawled,
They've moved on, but
Imagine their sound . . .

If we could hear it
When their feet fell
What would it sound like?
What stories could it tell?

The boom of a bear paw,
The slither of a snake,
The whisper of a whisker
Sifting like a rake

The jump of a jackrabbit,
Scurry of a mouse
The barely-there pinpricks of
a moth near the house

The clack of a crab claw,
The clip-clop of a horse,
The friendly furry paw
of a dog (of course)

The trot of a turkey,
The gallop of a goose,
The duck's waddling wandering,
Birds skitter loose

Lean in closely,
Examine what you see
You might just imagine it,
this sandy symphony.

PONDER

Many animals are nocturnal, which means they are awake at night and sleep during the day. Can you imagine what that would be like? It's an amazing mystery that lets us share some of the same places with animals. We might have a favorite place to take our walks during the day, and at night it might be a mouse's favorite place to scurry about! When we look for animal prints, we get to be detectives, searching for clues about animals that share this space with us—at night or at other times. What a good design, that God made us able to share this world like that!

PRAY

Lord, how interesting that you chose to create life, the earth, and science in such a way that footprints would be possible. As we look at footprints, paw prints, or any other sort of prints today, help us to marvel at your good design in giving every creature a purpose, a place, and a time . . . including us! When people look at the marks we leave behind with our choices and lives each day, we pray that we would be a blessing to others by helping wherever we can and filling our hearts with your joy.

PLAY ....

Footprint Match

Pull out your magnifying glasses and take a close look around you. If you don't see any naturally occurring animal tracks, you could create some with a stick in the shape of creatures' tracks. Ask some Curiosity Questions (see Further Resources) to help kids notice details. Then ask, "What type of animal do you think this belongs to?" Invite interaction by asking kids to show what the animal walks like (they can mimic), or what sorts of motions or noises they make. Ask, "What could someone tell by looking at *your* tracks?" To finish with a burst of activity, give kids a mission: create the craziest track of footprints that you can while running. Ready . . . set . . . *go!*

PAIR ....

Pizzicato from *Sylvia*

Léo Delibes

⁓

You bring darkness, it becomes night,
and all the beasts of the forest prowl . . .
. . . The sun rises, and they steal away;
they return and lie down in their dens.

Psalm 104:20, 22 niv

FINDING A FEATHER

Fluttering feather,
Where have you flown?
In what sort of weather?
What skies have you known?

Once wind whispered through you,
You soared through the sky
Once sunbeams came to you
On wings flying high

Feather aflutter,
So soft and so fine
When skies start to sputter
Your colors still shine

Keeping safe, keeping warm
A bird in the air
In a cloud, in a storm
As it flew way up there

Fluttering feather,
You've drifted on down
Like a faraway letter
Bringing news to the ground

PONDER

See how a feather looks like it's made of a thousand tiny threads?
These make something very soft into something very strong too!
They lock together, a lot like your fingers when you fold your hands

together, making things extra tight and warm for safety, and mighty for movement and flight. Gentle things can be strong too!

PRAY

Jesus, a simple thing like a feather is not simple at all! You've created it to keep birds safe and warm, to let them fly, and to let us discover them and imagine all these wonderful things. If you care for birds so very well, we know that you will always care for us too. Thank you for feathers!

PLAY

Feather Drop (hands-on option)

Using the feather you've discovered, and a few other found objects from nearby (twig, pebble, tissue from your bag, glove, etc.), drop items two by two to see what falls to the ground faster, and to notice together different ways that things fall.

To expand the wonder, do an internet search for a short video (just over a minute) called "NASA Apollo 15 Hammer-Feather Drop" and see what happens when an astronaut drops these two objects on the moon! Let kids guess what will happen, then watch the video.

Depending on your child's readiness, discuss why it's different on the moon versus on earth. On earth, we have air, which is like an invisible sea for the feather to float down through, slowing it down. On the moon, there's no air (a vacuum), so it falls directly down—at the same speed as the hammer!

Feathers can carry bacteria, so be sure to wash your hands well after handling your fluttering treasure.

Feather Spray (no touch option)

Using a water spray bottle, let kids spray the feather to observe what the water does. It will likely bead up into droplets. Lead them in inquiring why that could be, and offering possible ideas or comparisons that might help them come up with ideas: "Why do you think umbrellas keep people dry?" (Shape, type of fabric, etc.) "Do you think any of that could be true for feathers?" Study the feather with a magnifying glass. Invite kids to share what they notice.

Against a backdrop of dirt, rock, concrete, or asphalt, spray the feather again thoroughly, including the ground or surface around it. Move the feather to reveal the dry place that's been left below. If it's on a hard surface, let the kids trace the dry shape with chalk. Or repeat the spraying process, this time using their hands as the barrier over the ground (instead of the feather), to reveal the shape of their hand when finished. Talk about how the water feels on their skin, and how the bird would feel if that water was all over its skin instead of on its feathers! Let kids have fun shaking the water off, flicking fingers to fling it off, and letting their hands dry.

PAIR

"Pas de Deux" from *The Nutcracker*

Pyotr Ilyich Tchaikovsky

~

*. . . those who hope in the LORD will renew their strength.
They will soar on wings like eagles; they will run and
not grow weary; they will walk and not be faint."*

ISAIAH 40:31 NIV

*Notice the tiny hooklets and barbs on the feathers. These make
something very soft into something very strong too!*

NEST

Newly and neatly and sweetly and swift, a bird will nest in spring

Easterly, westerly, south she soars and dives and flits her wings

Swoop and dip and swoop again, a thousand times to bring

Twigs and feathers, grass and leaves, and bits and bobs and string

PONDER

Birds build their nests out of all kinds of things! Certain kinds of birds build one small sprig at a time; they gather blades of grass, pieces of fluff, straw, string, and more. They work and work until they've built something both strong and soft . . . all with little "left-over" material everyone else overlooks. It's like a treasure hunt! God has placed treasures all around us and provides for His creation in all kinds of ways.

PRAY

God, thank you for giving the birds everything they need to build a home. Your Word tells us that if you care for the birds, you will also care for our every need! Thank you that we are safe with you, no matter what.

PLAY

Gathered Home

Find a place with natural resources (sticks, grass, trees, leaves, etc.) where you feel comfortable doing a little exploring together. Set some boundaries for where to stay and issue the challenge: Build a shelter using only things you gather from what you see. You may also wish to give each person some lengths of twine or masking tape as starting materials. Build one shelter together, pair off, or build individually. Shelters can be as simple (a clearing in grass) or complex (a lean-to of sticks against trees) as you like. Talk about the challenges and delights of building a gathered home (as birds do with nests). For extra fun, let kids enjoy a snack or book in their new hideaways.

PAIR

Petite Suite de Concert, Op. 77: III. "Un Sonnet d'Amour"

Samuel Coleridge-Taylor

Even the sparrow finds a home,
and the swallow a nest for herself,
where she may lay her young . . .

PSALM 84:3 ESV

*An **acrostic** poem uses the first letter of each line to spell something. Can you see what the acrostic above spells?*

GROWING
THINGS

DANDELION

PAUSE..

Cloud of fluff on a stem
Take a big breath and then

Blow it hard! Blow it quick!
Small umbrellas on a stick—

They take flight, dance and swirl,
They spread out, dip and twirl

And then onward they go
On a journey to and fro

Where they burrow in the ground
Plant new life, safe and sound.

PONDER..

Isn't it incredible to think that one little flower can turn into so many new ones? Each one of those "umbrellas on a stick" that released when you blew on the dandelion is a seed, and every single one can grow a whole new flower. Imagine all of the new life that will come just because of that one!

Do you know what else does that? Your smile! When you smile at others, notice how a lot of times, they smile right back. And then they might smile at someone else, and that new someone might smile too. . . . Who knows how far one smile can go, on a journey to and fro! God created joy to spread.

PRAY ....

Lord, how amazing that a single dandelion can plant so many new ones! Thank you for creating things that bring us delight and wonder, and that invite us to be a part of helping joy to grow.

PLAY ....

Dandelion Outline

Tear out a blank page from your nature journal. Using a stick or pencil, carefully poke holes in the paper in a fun design (swirl, smiley face, flower), or in the shape that creates the first letter of your child's name. Invite your child to pick as many dandelions as they can find, whether white and fluffy or yellow and blooming. Insert the stems into each hole you created, so that your design is now populated by dandelion heads.

If there are fluffy white ones included in your design, take a big breath together and collectively blow to release the seeds of your whole design!

Dandelion Dip

Pick a dandelion that is at the white, fluffy stage of its life. Fill a glass container with water, then carefully take turns dipping the dandelion slowly, headfirst, into the water. Slowly pull it out and be amazed: It will be dry and fully intact!

Dandelion Garland

Dandelions bloom yellow, then close for many days before opening into their white fluff. Hunt for dandelions in their closed-up stage. Pick their heads and carefully string together using needle and thread, or gently spear them onto a wire. Space them out along the thread or wire, display the garland or shape the wire into a circle to create a wreath, and wait several days for them to begin opening into their fluffy white balls. As a final hurrah, take the garland/wreath out somewhere you feel comfortable releasing seeds, and watch them fly as you whirl the creation around.

PAIR..

"Csárdás"

Vittorio Monti

(Especially starting at the two-minute mark)

~

A glad heart makes a cheerful face . . .

PROVERBS 15:13a ESV

WHEN LIGHT DANCES THROUGH TREES

PAUSE..

Green trees
with shimmering leaves
and sunspots shining through
Reach high
into the sky
with shade for me and you

A dance of light
a skitter so bright
from a star very far away
Watch it dash
and flicker and splash
inviting you to play.

PONDER..

That tree grew so high, didn't it? All because of its roots so deep, drinking water from the soil down below. Something that roots so deep into the earth is also reaching up high into the sky with its tree limbs and leaves, making light all the way from the sun dance around on you. The sun is the star closest to earth . . . so you're playing with starlight! We see trees all the time, so it can be easy to forget that they're pretty miraculous. They grip the earth with their roots, the sky with their branches, and starlight with their leaves—all to offer strength, shade, and shelter to others. Did you know we can do this too? We can root deep into God's Word, reach high into His love, and grow strong in doing both!

PRAY ....

God, thank you for letting us see starlight all the way from the sun play with the dancing leaves today. It reminds us that you have tucked light all around us—and you've made us to shine bright with your love.

PLAY ....

Ground Mural

Using sidewalk chalk from your adventure kit, or using lines of pebbles, twigs, small leaves, or other found objects around you, trace the shadow of the tree or leaves. On unpaved ground, you can use a stick or your finger to trace the outline into the dirt. Talk about it together: "What's your favorite leaf that you traced?" "Who do you think might see our drawing later? Let's pray for them, that they will notice beauty here too."

PAIR ....

"La campanella"

Franz Liszt

⁓

Blessed is the person who obeys the law of the LORD.
. . . the law of the LORD gives them joy . . .
That kind of person is like a tree that is planted near a stream of water.
It always bears its fruit at the right time.
Its leaves don't dry up.

PSALM 1:1–3 NIRV

PAUSE...

Down in the ground
Where you can't hear a sound
There's a silent symphony

With a tap-tap-tap
Tiny roots make a track
On a pebble timpani

And they turn and they twist
And they grip like a fist
Holding soil like a living net

With a trundle-tumble-ting
And a splish-splosh-sing
They tunnel their notes where it's wet

Like a fiddle-fiddle-fling
of the violin strings
they map their silent song

Where the roots twirl steep
And it's dark, and it's deep
We won't be waiting long

A glimpse comes first,
A tiny green burst
From that secret work down below

Then it's up, up, up!
Through the mud and the muck
Toward the sun's bright shining glow.

PONDER..

Roots start out tiny and are even soft to touch. But it's these tiny, hidden things that make a plant strong, keep it from blowing away, and let it soak in the water from the earth. How wonderful to see that tiny things can be so strong and important! God's Word even tells us, "Do not despise these small beginnings, for the LORD rejoices to see the work begin . . ." (Zechariah 4:10 NLT).

PRAY ....

God, you care very much about small beginnings and work that is done in places only you can see. When we are growing or doing hidden work for good things, help us to take heart and know that life can come from places like that. That even when we feel like nobody sees, you see, and it makes your heart glad.

PLAY ....

Root Study

- Look up a time-lapse video online of roots growing and share with your kids.
- In a transparent container like a jar, plant some grass seeds in soil so that your kids can watch the growth underground, as well as above. Invite them to help water the seeds and find a sunny spot for them. Use nature journals to sketch each week and talk about what looks different or interesting together. If the grass gets long enough, cut some and let them make interesting shapes with it on paper, or form letters to spell their name. Tape or glue it down.
- Find a weed that you would pull anyway. Carefully uproot it and examine the root system.

- For fun that's a bit messier, let kids dig in the mud, pretending they're a root tunneling down.
- To show kids a timpani in action, find a video of a live orchestra playing "Sunrise Fanfare" by Richard Strauss. Let kids play along by giving them empty paper towel tubes to drum along on pillows with all their might.

PAIR

Waltz No. 2 from Jazz Suite No. 2

Dmitri Shostakovich

Enjoy the way the melody is carried atop the driving treble piano, resembling the way something deep down (roots) supports the life above.

And I will give you treasures hidden in the darkness—
secret riches.
I will do this so you may know that I am the LORD,
the God of Israel, the one who calls you by name.

ISAIAH 45:3 NLT

A **timpani** is a kind of drum!
A **symphony** is a beautiful song played by many instruments all together.

LIFE IN A CRACK IN A SIDEWALK

There's a rock-hard place
In the pavement by the road
Where the ground's so tough
That nothing can grow.

Where the cars whiz by,
People's shoes clip-clop
Where the sun glows hot
And the seeds won't drop.

"We can't grow here!"
they proclaim with a frown
"It's scary and it's fast—
The worst place in town!"

But a little seed lands
in a crack right there
And it burrows deep down,
Too busy to stay scared.

It roots and it sprouts
Then it grows up tall
'til a little flower blooms,
Beautiful and small.

Its bright head bobs
On the wind dancing through
Other seeds sail by
thinking, "Look what we could do!"

A girl walks past
And spots the sunny bloom
In the busy sidewalk
As the cars still zoom

It brings her a smile
As she kneels down low,
Sees the crack and thinks,
"Look how broken places grow!"

PONDER

It sure seems impossible for a tiny seed to be able to grow in such a hard place, doesn't it? That sidewalk (or street, parking lot, etc.) is so hard that even great big people don't fall through it! But look how a small seed was able to grow there, all because of a crack.

Remember, just because something is hard doesn't mean it's impossible. And even though something might be cracked or broken, sometimes that broken place allows new life to grow!

PRAY

God, sometimes we find ourselves in hard places. Thank you that you are right there with us! You will give us strength to grow there, and never leave us, not even for a second. Help our lives show this to others, so that they might smile with hope, just like the girl in the poem.

PLAY

Nature Weave

Tear out a page from your nature journal. Fold it in half vertically. Guide kids in making a tear or cut across the folded edge horizontally, stopping about an inch from the vertical outside edges. Continue this in parallel cuts all the way down the page, in strips about an inch apart. Unfold it, and voila—a nature loom!

Have kids gather long pieces of grass, sprigs, flowers, dandelions, twigs, leaves, clovers, etc. If you're not in a growth season geographically, dried bits of nature will work too. Using their "harvest," weave the nature elements into the loom. Discuss how because of the "cracks" in the paper, they were able to create a beautiful work of art!

At home, you can press the woven art in between heavy books (sandwiching the art between parchment, wax paper, or other paper) until dry. Or simply display until the art has run its course.

PAIR..

Siete canciones populares españolas: IV. "Jota"
Manuel de Falla (arr. Paul Kochanski)

If I lie down in the deepest parts of the earth, you are also there.
PSALM 139:8B NIRV

4-line rhyming stanzas are called **quatrains***. Can you find other poems in this book containing quatrains?*

GRASS

Crawling, sprawling jungle where sky weaves itself through land
Rolling, scrolling sunlit stage where breeze and light enchant
Waving, swaying reaching tips, adventure here awaits
Tickling, prickling carpet for this starlit barefoot dance

PONDER

Grass is incredible! Sometimes we see it so often that we forget to notice that a great green universe is springing up from brown soil, transforming a hard place into something soft. Hold out your palm and brush it over the grass. . . . Do you feel how gentle it is? It's like a whisper over your skin. (Invite kids to whisper the word *whisper* as they run their palm along the tips of the grass). Thousands and thousands of grass seeds sprout into grass blades to grow this living carpet for you.

PRAY

God, thank you for making grass. You used one of the tiniest seeds in the world to transform it in one of the biggest ways! You make life grow where there was none, and make a hard place soft, all through the work of these tiny seeds. Thank you for using small things to do great big things.

PLAY

Based on your comfort level, the following can be experienced with or without shoes on. If kids have shoes off, ask them, "How does the grass feel on your feet?" and talk about it for a multisensory experience. Be careful of bees, thorns, rocks, etc. (See Wonder in the Wild in Further Resources at the end of this book for how to coach kids through spotting potential hazards.)

Treasure Hunt

Have kids look for the following in the grass:

A thick grass blade
A thin grass blade
A clover
A yellow dandelion
A white and fluffy dandelion
A leaf
A bug (they can leave it where it is)
A sunny spot
A shady spot

They can call out when they find it. Skip irrelevant items, and feel free to add in other items that are present wherever you are. Afterward, free play with running, zigzagging, crab-walking, somersaults, cartwheels, spinning, skipping, or a game of tag.

PAIR..

Frühlingsstimmen ("Voices of Spring"), Op. 410

Johann Strauss II

(Challenge kids to match the speed of their running/
playing to the music when it goes extra fast.)

~

*If that is how God clothes the grass of the field . . . will he not much
more clothe you . . . ? So do not worry, saying, "What shall we eat?"
or "What shall we drink?" or "What shall we wear?" For . . . your
heavenly Father knows that you need them.*

MATTHEW 6:30–34 NIV

*A poem where words create a picture (like the rolling grassy
hills formed by the lines of this poem) is called a **concrete
poem**. To try one, sketch an outlined image in pencil. Then,
write your words atop in pen. Once the ink is dry, erase the
pencil lines beneath. Enjoy your concrete poem!*

ALONG THE WAY

WHEN AN OBSTACLE IS AHEAD

When the road ahead is bumpy
Or a hill too big to climb
If you're starting to feel grumpy
Just remember this small rhyme:

You don't have to scale a mountain
Or leap across the lake,
If you're feeling like you're bound, then
Just one step you can take

Just one step will bring you nearer
Just one step will pave the way
And the way will become clearer
As you seize the day.

That one step leads to another,
And another, and one more
Just a little farther and
Soon your heart will soar

The path is all behind you, see?
Turn and take a look—
You completed this whole journey
Since one step you took!

PONDER

When something ahead looks hard, steep, or bumpy, it's easy for us to think, "That hill is bigger than me! It's going to be too hard." But you know what? God made that hill, and He made you too, and He'll be with you every step of the way. With His help, we can do hard things. At the end of the journey, we'll marvel at how we got to see and do amazing things. Take courage! You can do this!

PRAY ....

Lord, when the road ahead looks too hard, I pray that you would help me feel your presence. Help me to know that you will never leave me. Help me to focus on just the next step with your strength, and help me to see your wonderful creation all along the way. Thank you for always being there to help us!

PLAY ....

If you're heading down a hill that you know you'll be returning upward on, give kids a piece of sidewalk chalk. On the way down, have them draw lines or pictures along the way. Then, on the return uphill climb, use those drawings as landmarks, saying things like "I know it seems like a long climb ahead, but let's just see if we can make it to the chalk line/drawing that's next." When you reach it, stop to celebrate! Rest if needed. Then, ask if anyone spots the next line or drawing, and begin the next leg of the journey.

If you're on a hill you didn't come down, modify this by taking turns picking mini-destinations. "Let's make it to the [pine cone, stick, fire hydrant, stop sign, etc.]." Take turns picking the next short-distance landmark and celebrate when you reach each one. Kids can collect small items that were used as landmarks, such as pebbles, pinecones, or twigs to add to your Wonder Jar back home.

PAIR..

"Promenade" (Walking the Dog)

George Gershwin

～

I lift up my eyes to the hills.
From where does my help come?
My help comes from the LORD,
who made heaven and earth.

PSALM 121:1–2 ESV

To celebrate the journey for those who may be seated in a wheelchair or stroller, replace the word "step" with "inch" in this poem.

WHEN JOY IS SHARED

Can you hear it in the air?

l^a u^g h^t e^r

comes after
someone had a smile

Can you see it spreading wide?

s   g
  m   n
    i   l   i

from piling

delight up deep inside

Can you feel it bubble up?

d e l i g h t   c a n

be bright and
wrap us up in joy

Can you feel the warming glow?

j o y   i s

a story that
invites our hearts to grow.

PONDER..

The Bible says that as we follow His path, He will grow our hearts! (Psalm 119:32). One of the ways of His path is to rejoice with those who rejoice (Romans 12:15). When we see someone experience something wonderful, like making a great discovery, or getting good news, or even opening a present, sometimes we wish it had been us. But guess what? Our hearts can be taught to take great joy simply at the fact that someone else is experiencing joy. What a gift! So when we see someone smile, or hear them laugh, or see their face brighten, let's give thanks for their joy today.

PRAY..

Jesus, you didn't have to make laughter, or smiles, or joy . . . but you did, and we thank you for that good creation. Thank you for the times when we experience it and thank you for the times when others do. Help us be happy at the happiness of others, and thank you for the chance to do that.

PLAY..

Smile Challenge

To illustrate how joy can be contagious, invite your kids to play a version of the staring game. The rules are that you look at each other, don't break eye contact, and try not to smile. You can make silly faces, you can hum or tell jokes, or you can be silent—and you wait to see who cracks a smile or laughs first. The best part is, as soon as they do, everyone else does too! Point this out at the end, and delight together over shared joy.

Bonus: Ask if there's someone on their heart who they would like to deliver joy to today. Pray and discuss ideas: Could you bring someone a bouquet of flowers? Bake someone cookies? Carry out your plan, watch the joy it brings . . . and the joy that it delivers to you too.

PAIR

"Ode to Joy" (piano version)

Ludwig van Beethoven

~

Rejoice with those who rejoice . . .

ROMANS 12:15 ESV

WHEN A PASSERBY FROWNS

PAUSE

Have you ever seen a sad someone
a frown upon their face
and wondered what your job might be
here within this place?

You don't have to make it all okay,
turn their frown into a smile,
but there's a reason that you passed this way
on this great big mile.

You might offer up a smallish wave,
a smile to cheer their day
You might offer them a treasure found,
discovered on the way.

Or you simply might just say a prayer,
A secret in your heart:
"God, please help them in their sadness;
They're your precious work of art."

PONDER

Sometimes when we see sadness, we might not know what to do. We wish we could make it all better for the person who is sad, but we're not sure how.

The wonderful news is . . . you're making a difference just by being there! Think of this: You might be the only person in the world praying for that person's sadness right this very moment. God knows just how to help that person, and He's helping them by inviting you to pray for them, and maybe even by doing a small something for them . . . which might feel to them like a great big something.

PRAY

Jesus, you are always there for us—in the good times and in the hard times. You've been through hard times yourself, and you know just how to draw near to someone whose heart is hurting. We pray for [fill in description: the person we saw today, the person's name, etc.] and trust that you will strengthen them when they feel sad. Please give them hope, and show us if there is something you would like us to do for them.

PLAY

Create Comfort

Has your sadness ever felt better when someone in your family wipes away your tears, gives you a warm hug, or sits with you to read or play for a while? That "better" feeling is called *comfort.*

We can help give comfort to those who are sad by letting them know we're thinking of them. One way of doing this is to create a card or picture for them. Take some time today to color, draw, or paint pictures or cards. You can write a hope-giving Bible verse on it too, if you'd like! Keep some of your creations in your adventure kit.

Next time you're out, pray for God to show you someone to give the gift of cheer or comfort. Together with your grown-up, decide who that could be, and choose one of your creations to give them. You can say something simple like, "Here you go. This is for you!"

PAIR

Piano Sonata No. 8 in C Minor, Op. 13
(*Sonata Pathétique*): II. Adagio cantabile

Ludwig van Beethoven

Blessed are those who are sad.
They will be comforted.

MATTHEW 5:4 NIRV

Verses that could work well to write on your creations:

. . . joy comes in the morning.

PSALM 30:5B NIRV

. . . but those who hope in the LORD
will renew their strength.
They will soar on wings like eagles;
they will run and not grow weary,
they will walk and not be faint.

ISAIAH 40:31 NIV

WHEN PLANS ARE INTERRUPTED

PAUSE

Plans are set, come on, let's go!
Then someone says, "Just wait—oh no!"

Someone's sick, or the weather's ick,
Help is needed, or roads are slick!

Your plans are crashed and your hopes are dashed
And the whole entire day feels smashed.

"Interruption?" Yes, it's true:
that sounds like what volcanoes do!

But just you wait—no exploding yet.
A change in plans . . . might just let

us see a new and different way
a strange adventure in our day.

Someone's sick? What can we bring?
The weather's ick? Ideas fling —

for inside fun—our plans can wait.
Our hopes aren't dashed—why, we can skate

on floors with socks, or build a fort,
or cut snowflakes, laugh 'til we snort

So your plans seem crashed and your great hopes too;
Take heart and see what you can do!

PONDER...

Have you been looking forward to something, and then something happened to stop it? That can feel so sad, and it's okay to feel disappointed. But then, you get to choose what to do with that disappointment: stay sitting in sadness, or ask, "What adventure could we have instead?" Asking that question can change your entire day. You could see or do something you never even planned or imagined, which could turn out to be the best adventure of all!

So, hang on, and ride this change of plans with excitement . . . I wonder what God has in store for us today?

PRAY ....

God, thank you that even when plans change, you never do. You're still a God who loves us and can give us a different plan than we imagined—one that's still so full of goodness, hope, purpose, and even joy. Please give us eyes to see the new adventure you have for us today.

PLAY ....

Lessons from Geodes

Geodes are rocks that look very plain and unremarkable on the outside, but once cracked open, reveal a treasure trove of sparkling crystals and color! Talk together about how this can be a lot like interruptions: They might look boring or even bothersome on the surface, but if we dig a little deeper, we can find the treasure of adventures, memories, and new journeys that we never would have otherwise found.

To make this a hands-on, teachable moment, buy a geode kit online or from a craft/hobby store and keep it tucked away to pull out when you have an interruption and use this entry. Or create your own geode craft by cutting an egg carton into its individual craters (leave hinged if possible, so each portion has a top and a bottom). Color or decorate the inside, and enjoy your colorful creations!

PAIR...

Symphony No. 94 in G Major Hob. I:94 (The Surprise Symphony): II. Andante

Joseph Haydn

Notice how the symphony, which has several notes that sound surprising, shifts tone shortly after the two-minute mark. Then, about thirty seconds later, it shifts again from this new ominous sound into something with a fresh liveliness. How is this a little like the interruptions that change our days in unexpected ways to give us unexpected adventures?

~

A man's heart plans his way,
But the LORD directs his steps.

PROVERBS 16:9 NKJV

WHEN YOU HEAR A SNATCH OF MUSIC

PAUSE...

Listen to these borrowed things
Plinked on pianos, plucked on strings
Piece of music passing by

as	*h*
notes	*g*
drift	*i*
d	*h*
o	*lifts*
w	*heart*
n	*my*

PONDER ....

Music is invisible, but it can fill a room, curl inside you, wrap your heart, and give joy, comfort, and peace. No one can see any of this, but often you can feel that something remarkable and amazing is happening! And here's something else incredible: If you look at the keys of a piano, you'll see that there are only so many notes there. The keyboard doesn't go on forever, does it? But even so, those notes are like puzzle pieces that have been put together a million different ways to make different songs for thousands of years . . . and they're still being used in brand-new ways to make entirely *new* songs too. Music is such a gift—and God gave us ears to hear it. He loves for us to enjoy the gifts He made for us . . . and we can use music to praise Him too!

PRAY

God, when we hear music playing, help us remember to take joy in the gift of it. You made it for us, you made us to enjoy it, and we praise you and thank you for this very good work. Please use music today to bless people in special ways.

PLAY

Nature's Instruments

Take a moment to watch and listen to your surroundings, whether in a yard, park, trail, playground, or other outdoor space. What do you see moving? What do you hear? Now, challenge kids to get creative and choose a "found instrument"—two sticks to clack together, a low-hanging branch of leaves to rattle, a pile of dry leaves to crunch, a tree trunk or other object to pat their hands on like a drum, or perhaps the instrument is their own voice or whistle. Play a favorite worship or just-for-fun song from your phone, or simply sing it together and invite kids to use their instruments to play along.

PAIR

25 Études Faciles et Progressives, Op. 100: VII.
"Le Courant Limpide"

Friedrich Burgmüller

~

*All the earth worships you
and sings praises to you;
they sing praises to your name.*

PSALM 66:4 ESV

WHEN FEAR COMES TO VISIT

PAUSE

There's a funny sometimes hidden thing,
My stomach feels all tied with string.
Or shivers running up my spine,
And everything's just not-quite-fine . . .

(you might say that I'm afraid)

So I feel like heading home right now,
I'm thinking, thinking, thinking, wow—
Of all the things that could go wrong
The list grows longer, longer, strong . . .

(you might say that I'm afraid)

But, God, you say you're stronger still;
I feel you ask me if I will
Invite you in and venture on
Find strength in you and we'll keep on . . .

(you might say I'm not alone)

And I'm growing, seeing, as I learn—
Fear comes my way but I can turn
And say I'll do it anyway:
The King of the world beside me stays!

(and with Him, I am brave)

So when I feel I'd like to hide
I turn my eyes on hope and light.
I want to live with you so bold,
This world of yours, bravely behold.

PONDER

Have you ever felt afraid? You're not the only one. Fear is no fun, but I promise you you're not alone. Lots of people feel afraid, for lots of different reasons. Whenever fears come, we might wish they'd just go away—but guess what? We can do something even better. We can take them to the God of the entire universe, who cares so much about everything we're facing. He even has some very helpful instructions for how to turn fear into peace!

PRAY

God, as we're adventuring and feel afraid of unexpected things, help us to take care and be safe, but also to remember that you have given us a spirit of boldness. Even when we don't feel brave, you can strengthen our hearts to take the next step. You made us to do great things—but you don't ask us to do them alone. You stay with us every step of the way, and give us everything we need. Thank you for being a God who is close!

PLAY

Transformation Art

Philippians 4:6–8 NIV gives beautiful instruction for how to transform worry, fear, and anxiety into peace:

"Do not be anxious about anything, but in every situation, by prayer and petition, with thanksgiving, present your requests to

God. And the peace of God, which transcends all understanding, will guard your hearts and your minds in Christ Jesus. Finally, brothers and sisters, whatever is true, whatever is noble, whatever is right, whatever is pure, whatever is lovely, whatever is admirable —if anything is excellent or praiseworthy—think about such things."

Together, list everything true, noble, right, pure, lovely, admirable, excellent, or praiseworthy that you see. For very young kids, you can simplify this by saying, "Let's list all of the amazing things we see, or all of the things around us that we like." This invites kids to shift their focus from fear to gratitude—not to ignore fear, but to place it securely with God, draw close to Him, and press on together.

For a visual representation of transforming fear, invite kids to create a colorful design with markers on a blank piece of paper. Then, color a thick layer of solid black crayon, and let kids use a coin's edge, pen cap, or other object to etch fun designs into the black layer, revealing life beneath. You can also save time by purchasing pre-made scratch-art pages.

PAIR

"Fanfare for the Common Man"

Aaron Copland

Note how the initial foreboding drums soon morph into a triumphant and courage-giving brass chorus.

⁓

I can do all things through Christ who strengthens me.

PHILIPPIANS 4:13 NKJV

WHEN YOU'RE WAITING

You're moving forward, having fun,
You're set to get some big things done!
You're on adventures, start to run—
When suddenly, you

stop.
w a i t .

The fun has stopped. No time to play—
There's something standing in the way.
Your happiness begins to fray
When warily,* you

stop.
w a i t .

You stand in line or wait to dine
or blink and think as stoplights shine.
And just before you start to whine
you . . .

w a i t.
stop.

What's that you see? That splendid thing—
You've spotted something int'resting
And there! And there! The wonders spring . . .
This stopping, waiting, joy can bring!

PONDER ....

Waiting can be hard, especially when we're on our way to something fun! But think of it this way: If you have to wait five minutes, would you rather wait five minutes happy? Or wait five minutes mad? Look at "waiting time" as hidden pockets of adventure. Some people say that over your whole entire life, if you add up all the time you spend waiting in lines or at stoplights, that time could add up to months or even years! How exciting that we get to choose how we spend all of our waiting time . . . and that if we choose to, we can spot joyful things right here while we wait too.

PRAY ....

God, you created times of waiting just like you created times of action. In fact, waiting can be an action too! Please help us see ways to make our times of waiting matter. You knew just where we would be in each moment you created. Thank you for the gift of time . . . and waiting!

PLAY ....

Redeem the Time

Choose one of these ways to fill your waiting time with fruitful things:

- **Look for a way to help:** Train your kids to go from observers to engaged helpers, and to grow a servant-hearted perspective. Wherever you're waiting, be on the lookout for ways to help. For example, did someone drop something while you were waiting at the store? If you feel the situation is safe, encourage your child to hand the item to that person. Another way to help is to use the time to pray together for someone.

- **Play "I Spot Something Int'resting"** (a re-imagined version of "I spy"): Take turns choosing something you see, hear, or smell. Say, "I spot something int'resting, and the color is _____." *or* "It sounds like _____." *or* "It smells like _____." Others in the group take turns guessing what it is. You can ask for one additional clue each at any point in the game.

PAIR

Symphony No. 8 in F Major, Op. 93: II.
Allegretto scherzando

Ludwig van Beethoven

Note how the instruments' rhythm
resembles the ticking of a clock.

Teach us to number our days,
that we may gain a heart of wisdom.

PSALM 90:12 NIV

*Warily means "I'm not so sure about this . . ."

SEASONS

FOUR SEASONS TREE BUDS

PAUSE..

Read each section during its own season, or all four together for a broad view of a tree's cycle.

SPRING

Springtime bud is a folded-in leaf,
tucked in its case,
miniature and brief.

Springtime bud warms in the sun,
loosens its grip,
slowly comes undone.

Springtime leaf unfolds its wrinkled crease
like a packed-up work of art,
spreading out its leafy reach.

Just wait . . .

SUMMER

Summer tree grows a tiny bud beneath
right at the base
of a lively green leaf.

Follow the stem to where it all began
like an arrow to the branch
imagine if you can.

In the leaf-dance above a lively tree's bark
the tree is preparing
for the winter's dark.

Just wait . . .

AUTUMN

Autumn buds can be easily found.
unveiled now
as leaves fall to the ground.

Twigs clack and clatter as a storm comes on
the buds remain
as the dizzy scene dawns.

Tiny little bumps don't appear like much is there,
inside is a treasure,
though the tree may be bare

Just wait . . .

WINTER

Winter bud is a capsule of hope.
glimpse of the future,
a tiny telescope.

A little leaf inside, like a safe, strong cocoon.
tree pauses its growth,
cold beneath the silver moon.

Protection is its purpose and promise is its song.
there is life kept inside,
in the winter, dark and long.

Just wait . . .

PONDER...

It takes each season for tree buds to create the life that they do, and
we can learn so much from that.

In the SPRING, the tree is working and growing, starting small in order to do big things.

In SUMMER, the tree is full of life! It gives shelter, strength, shade, and a place to play.

In FALL, the tree releases its leaves in a show of beauty, joy, and preparation for the next season.

In WINTER, the tree is resting, protecting the life the buds are storing up for springtime.

Work, growth, play, sharing joy, rest . . . these are all very good creations of God. For trees, and for us too!

PRAY

God, thank you that you have life packed up inside these tiny bundles called buds, and that they sprout into leaves that give shade, dance in the sun, and clap together in the wind. Thank you for the way trees teach us that waiting can lead to such good things.

PLAY

Spy on the Season (All Four Seasons)

Paying close attention to a single, same tree at different times of year (or even different times of day!) can reveal a hidden universe of life. Read each "bud" poem in its respective season and invite children to color, sketch, paint, or take a picture of the same tree in each season. Once you have more than one seasonal sketch, take some time to admire the differences and similarities you can spot together between them. For older kids, extend this activity by creating a Venn diagram and filling it in with colorful words and pictures.

Twig Maze (Autumn, Winter, Spring)

Gather twigs that have fallen to the ground. Examine buds together, then use the twigs to create the edges of a maze or meandering path. For younger kids, provide more guidance by drawing a line in the dirt and asking them to lay sticks upon it. For older kids, allow them to be a part of determining where the path/maze goes. When it's done, have fun traversing its course together. Do it once walking, once running, once hopping, once skipping, etc. Talk about how just like you're making your way through the path, life is slowly making its way through the branches above!

PAIR..

SPRING: *Appalachian Spring:*
VII. Doppio Movimento

Aaron Copland

SUMMER: *Capriccio espagnol,*
Op. 34: III. "Alborada"

Nikolai Rimsky-Korsakov

AUTUMN: Solfeggio in C minor, Hob. 220

Carl Philipp Emanuel Bach

WINTER: Concerto No. 4 in F Minor, Op. 8, RV 297
("Winter"): Allegro non molto

Antonio Vivaldi

For everything there is a season, and a time for every matter under heaven: . . . a time to break down, and a time to build up . . .

ECCLESIASTES 3:1, 3B ESV

A bud is like a tiny bundle, where the tree forms a miniature leaf that is folded up to fit in such a small space. The way it's folded is called **ptyxis** ("tix-iss"), and it's unique for each type of tree! To see a bud as described in this poem, check out the species of tree called the **live oak**.

FIRST GREEN

Grey world, little bud
How small, how strong! Season-hinge.
Little bud, green world . . .

PONDER

A hinge is something on which heavy things hang and turn. A door has hinges, and when you open it, you're in a whole new place! After a long winter, when you spot the first tiny traces of green in blades of grass or other plants and leaves, it's like the seasons are turning on a hinge: winter to spring. Soon, you'll step into a whole new world, painted with colorful life!

PRAY

Thank you, Lord, that great big changes can come through tiny things. When we see the earth come to life in the springtime, we thank you for the gift of hope, and how every small thing matters.

PLAY

Now-and-Later Painting

Fold a blank piece of paper in half, then unfold it again. Label the left side of the paper *Now* and the right side of the paper *Later*. Invite kids to paint (or sketch or color or take a crayon-rubbing of) the scene or "first green" item before them as it looks now. Then, talk together about how over time, more and more things will turn green, begin to bloom, grow taller and wider. Imagine together what the scene before you might look like when that happens, then invite them to fill in the *Later* half of the page with their imaginings.

PAIR

String Quintet in C Major, Op. 30, No. 6, G. 324
("La musica notturna delle strade di Madrid"):
IV. Allegro vivo, "Los Manolos"

Luigi Boccherini

~

I am about to do something new.
It is beginning to happen even now.
Don't you see it coming? . . .

ISAIAH 43:19 NIRV

*This poem is a **haiku,** a traditional Japanese form of poetry that usually . . .*

- *Has 3 lines (5 syllables, 7 syllables, 5 syllables)*
- *Includes nature themes*
- *Doesn't rhyme*

Try creating one together. The haiku's loveliness lies in its simplicity!

SPRING MACHINES

(AN ODE TO TRACTORS)

PAUSE...

Rusty corners,
Great big wheels
Rumbling motors rumble

Creaking hinges,
Big old pipes,
Tumbling dirt clods tumble

With metal scoops and bolts and bits,
Your strong work builds a form
For walls to rise and roofs to sit
A refuge from the storms

Crackling fires,
Pages turning,
Laughing voices sing

Sparkling thoughts
And words that move
Dreaming dreamers dream

While some are builders,
Some plant seeds
Plowing through the dirt

Working fields
and growing food
Bringing life from earth

Scrapers, backhoes,
Combines too,
Digger-shovels digging

Excavators
And Bobcats,
It's hope that you're creating!

PONDER

What a sight to see! Big machines moving ancient dirt in brand-new ways. Present, past, and future, all sitting together in the scene before you. Did you know that just like these tractors, the things we do today can make a great big difference tomorrow? They move earth to create buildings to live or work in, and fields to grow food. They are working hard to create things for others. Your actions and words can build too—things like joy and hope!

PRAY

Dear Lord, thank you for the chance to build! Whether we're making a tower with blocks, a house with tractors, or a smile out of words, it's a gift to be a part of creating. Thank you for being our Creator, and for the chance to be a part of that work. Please bless the people running the tractors today!

PLAY

Miniature Build

Invite kids to observe what the tractors are doing. Together, mimic the movements on a smaller level in the earth wherever you are, using found items around you. For example, use a stick to draw a square in the earth to represent the lot of land the tractors are working on. Kids can find a pebble or rock or thick twig to be their "tractor." They can plow, dig, lay twigs or blades of grass in the shape of a foundation or rows of a planted field, insert twigs upright into the ground to mimic the form of a house's frame, etc. Keep it as basic or detailed as you'd like. For a simpler rendition, let kids just draw what they see in the sand, using a finger or stick.

PAIR..

Le Carnaval des Animaux, V. "L'éléphant"

Camille Saint-Saëns

———

Therefore encourage one another and build up one another, just as you are doing.

1 Thessalonians 5:11 esv

FULL BLOOM

Sunny summer sunshine
Grass growing green
Fancy flowers look fine
Clothed as kings and queens

Clutch of catching color,
Symphony of sound
Windy waltz of wildflowers
Bend and dip and bow

Blooming blossoms bouncing
Fully flouncing forth
Summer's on your shoulders
Winter's in your warmth

PONDER

Look at this bright, blooming world of summer. There are miracles all around! Just think—all those months of winter, cold and colorless, are what helped make the summer color possible! Many plants need that season of rest, or a certain number of cold days before they can grow. So when you're looking at the full bloom of summer, you're also looking at the work and rest of winter.

PRAY

God, thank you for making every season full of purpose and full of its own kind of beauty. Help us remember in the middle of wintery times that summer is coming soon . . . and there's work being done all along to make the beauty possible. Thank you for being the giver of good gifts.

PLAY ....

Color Capture

Gather an assortment of colorful, non-toxic leaves, grasses, and flowers. On a hard, flat surface such as pavement or a cutting board protected by wax paper or plastic wrap, arrange them artfully atop a page of watercolor paper (for absorption). Lay paper towels over the top, then taking any precautions needed to guard against smashed fingers, gently tap a hammer over every part of every leaf, repeating as needed, releasing each leaf's pigment into the paper below. Remove paper towels and leaves to enjoy the pigment art on the paper below! Results will vary based on leaf type; you may wish to repeat the project once you have seen which leaves or flowers worked best for you. For extra fun, make your imprint into a greeting card, wall hanging, or wrapping paper.

PAIR ....

Pinocchio: II. "Verso l'avventura"

Alexander Litvinovsky

~

. . . for behold, the winter is past;
the rain is over and gone.
The flowers appear on the earth,
the time of singing has come . . .

SONG OF SOLOMON 2:11–12A ESV

CAMPFIRE

PAUSE

Hear that snap,
That split, that crack,
That pop from sap
Steaming

Orange, red, blue—
display each hue
A show for you
and me.

Sparks in the night
Twirl with starlight
Bursts glowing bright
and free

Shadows fling and
embers sing and
glowing zings
cozy

Warmth from a tree
That is older than me
shines light enchant-
ingly

PONDER

Did you know that trees can take from twenty to fifty years (or more!) to grow to their full size? There are many different reasons a tree gets chosen for firewood, but almost always, the logs in a campfire are older than you are.

All through its life, light poured down on that tree from the sun, growing it strong and tall. Animals scampered about, bees or other bugs explored it, birds may have nested in it. It stood through windy gusts and stormy nights, soaked in rain from so many clouds . . . and now, in the last bit of its story, it's giving the gift of warmth and light to you. It started with light and ends with light. How amazing is that?

As we enjoy this firelight, we can take strength from the fun and memories, and go out to shine into the world too! By giving gifts of kindness, friendship, love, help, and prayers, we can help warm the hearts of others.

PRAY

Lord, you made trees beautiful in every part of their life. Thank you that here, around the campfire, we get to be warm and happy because of all the seasons and storms this tree once stood through. Help make us strong through the storms to offer light to others.

PLAY

Discuss fire safety and set proximity rules that work best for your group.

Campfire in a Clap

Sit around the campfire (or near it, if you'd like more distance for safety). Choose one person to be the leader. Explain that the leader's job is to change noises every now and then (clapping, stomping, shuffling feet, clicking, whispering "pop," snapping or saying "snap," flicking fingers in a spark-like noise, pattering hands on knees, rubbing palms together, making *whoosh*-ing wind noise, etc.). Everyone else's job is to join the leader in every sound, paying close attention to when the leader changes, and copying them closely. Demonstrate possible noises, then get started! The result is a gradually shifting chorus of noises that mimics a campfire scene.

Take turns being leader, and feel free to introduce other noises into the rotation as well.

Sweet Treats (create for or with kids)

- **S'mores:** roasted marshmallows sandwiched between graham crackers or other cookies, along with part of a favorite candy bar of choice
- **Campfire cones:** empty ice cream cones filled with mini marshmallows, chocolate chips, berries, etc., then wrapped in foil/parchment and warmed near fire
- **Campfire éclairs:** croissant dough triangles wrapped around wooden dowel, "baked" by holding the croissant end of the stick over the fire. Slide off dowel when golden-brown, then fill with pudding and/or whipped cream.

PAIR

Sonata No. 1 in G minor, BWV 1001

Johann Sebastian Bach

(The guitar version lends a campfire feel!)

~

No one lights a lamp and puts it in a place where it will be hidden, or under a bowl. Instead they put it on its stand, so that those who come in may see the light.

LUKE 11:33 NIV

FALL OF LEAVES

PAUSE..

In the form of "Jabberwocky" by Lewis Carroll

[For younger adventurers, find the simplified poem-within-the-poem by reading only the **bold blue** words aloud.]

> 'Twas **autumn**, and the lively **leaves**
>   Did **toss** and tumble **in** the **breeze**:
> Kaleidoscope, **sunlight** receives
>   And **flings** colors **with ease**.
>
> "Observe the fall of leaves, my friend!
>   The tumble, fancy-free!
> Observe the twirling dance descend;
>   scattered happily!"
>
> **Winsome whispers**, hullabaloo;
>   hush and **hopes unfold**—
> Bright and bold, **bobbing** too
>   **Brought** on **from** the **cold**.
>
> And in the fine festivity
>   We scoop and toss and spin,
> Ruffling rain on lollygag lane
>   A lickety-split leaf grin . . .
>
> Hustle-bustle! Hurry-scurry!
>   The crispy twigs went **clicky-clack**!
> **Rat-a-tat**, then starts a flurry
>   The **wind blows branches back**.

*"And have you spun in the **shivering shock,***
   Shenanigans shuffling 'round?
O shining day! ***It's fall o'clock!***
   There's art upon the ground."

'Twas autumn, and the lively leaves
   Did toss and tumble in the breeze:
Kaleidoscope, sunlight receives
   And flings colors with ease.

PONDER

Did you know that trees eat too? Only instead of putting food in mouths, their leaves contain something very special (and *very* green) called chlorophyll that turns sunlight into energy, which helps trees grow and stay healthy . . . just like food does for you. Pretty amazing, right? After summertime, when the days get shorter, the trees make less chlorophyll. With less green covering them up from the inside, the leaves show all sorts of other colors that have been inside all along: red, orange, yellow, brown. We can take joy in getting to see these hidden treasures being revealed.

PRAY

Jesus, you call us "the light of the world." Thank you that we get to catch light too, by spending time with you. Thank you for the hidden color you have placed inside each leaf, like a treasure that comes out to light up the days just when they begin to grow darker.

PLAY

Forest-Floor Art

Gather an assortment of beautiful leaves and twigs. For an extra burst of action, count to ten while kids scurry as fast as they can to do so. Clear an area from the ground to use as your "canvas." Then place your treasures in an interesting pattern or scene. Snap a picture with your phone for the memory if you like, then leave your display there for someone else to find. Your light-catcher art will bring light to their day!

PAIR

"Humoresque"

Antonín Dvořák

You are the light of the world. . . .
Let your light shine before others,
so that they may see your good works
and give glory to your Father who is in heaven.

Matthew 5:14–16 esv

*A poem inspired by an existing poem is called an **after-poem**. Give it a try! Find a poem you like, then use its structure to write your own. Be sure to change the words and themes, and always credit the original with a phrase like "Inspired by _____" or "In the form of _____."*

MIGRATION

It's a marvelous myst'ry, the birds up there;
Ev'ry fall they take off and they fly through the air

Not just an inch or a jump-hop-skip . . .
These small, courageous creatures take a great big trip

Of miles and feathers and of feathers and miles . . .
Do they know, down below, that they're making us smile?

For they hardly packed a thing—just themselves, and their wings
They don't even have a sweater or a blanket to bring!

They'll soar over mountains and swoop through storms
Like a sigh as they fly, chasing sun and warmth

They're kings of the air, but they have no thrones;
Just their beaks, and techniques, and their small hollow bones

They ride on hurricanes and they slice through clouds
But they hardly weigh a thing and they aren't very loud

And they fly and they soar and their wings whisper-roar
As they climb and they swoop to see what's in store

Feet without ground and trip without map
They'll cross over countries and hear thunder clap!

"Impossible" journey? The answer is yes—
But also, the truth is: God made them for this!

PONDER..

When cold weather is on its way, some types of birds, butterflies, and other animals take off to find a warmer place to spend the winter. How do they know when to leave and how to get there—even if they've never gone before and are on their own? Scientists have some great ideas, but nobody knows for sure! It's a beautiful mystery. When you look at a bird, does it seem like something that small could make a journey across thousands of miles, or even entire oceans? It might seem impossible . . . and yet God built them with everything they need to do it. When you see the birds flying south in the winter, take heart! God gives you strength for your journeys too.

PRAY ....

God, thank you that you created birds with everything they need to make great big journeys that might sometimes seem too hard for them. Thank you for giving us everything we need for the journey of our life too! Help us ask you for strength when we need it, and to see your wonders everywhere we go. Amen.

PLAY ....

Mini-Migration

At an open space in a park, yard, or a nature trail, explain that birds migrate for two main connected reasons: temperature and food. Tell kids to take a good look all around them, and list together some of the things they notice (grass, picnic tables, pine cones, swings, leaves, etc.). Using the things they noticed, give them an imagination challenge, and they get to run and flap their wings all the way to the destination.

Pretend you're a bird that loves to eat grass! Where would you migrate to right now? Go! (Kids run to grassy patch)

Pretend you're a bird that likes to perch on swing sets. Where would you migrate? Go! (Kids run to swings, let them have fun "flying" [swinging])

Pretend you're a bird that builds their nests out of twigs and leaves. Where would you migrate? Go, and make a nest! (Kids run to twigs/leaves on ground. Invite them to heap materials into a "nest.")

Continue the game as long as you like, using the resources and locations available.

PAIR

"Farewell to Stromness"

Peter Maxwell Davies

~

. . .with God all things are possible.

MATTHEW 19:26B ESV

Have you seen the way geese migrate in V formation? Being the leader of the V is the most work, so the geese take turns in that spot so they each have a chance to rest and get their strength back. Rest is an important part of big journeys!

PUFF OF BREATH IN COLD AIR

PAUSE

Heave a happy huff of air
Put a puffy poof up there

Furling foggy frigid breath
Happens when there's no heat left

In the clatter-cloudy-cold
A timeless story told.

Veil of vapor, vanish clear
Misty moisture disappears

PONDER

When we breathe out, the air is very warm, just like you are, deep down in your lungs near your heart. Try breathing on your hand. Feel how warm it is? When the air outside is cold, the tiny bits of moisture in your breath that are usually invisible suddenly appear like little clouds!

When you get to see the invisible become suddenly visible—or the *unseen* become suddenly *seen*—it reminds us that in our lives, God is doing so much more than we can see with our eyes.

PRAY

Lord, even though we can't see you, we know you're always with us . . . like how even when we can't see our own breath, it's there! Thank you for the reminder that you are always with us, giving us life.

PLAY ....

Mist Art

Using the magnifying glass from your adventure kit, a small mirror, or a window/mirror in your home, invite kids to create steam on the glass by breathing out slowly. Then, they can have fun drawing designs or pictures in their "cloud" and watching it disappear! Feel free to invite them to be a part of cleaning the glass afterward if you like.

PAIR...

Le Carnaval des Animaux, VII. "Aquarium"

Camille Saint-Saëns

*Faith is being sure of what we hope for.
It is being sure of what we do not see.*

Hebrews 11:1 nirv

The start-of-word consonant sounds in this poem move from harsh to soft. Have some fun with this together in cold air; those closer to the beginning of the poem should produce some cloudy puffs, while the clouds may become smaller or invisible as you move into the softer sounds to close out the poem.

FROST

Step inside a frosted world,
you're stepping into two!
That tree you know,
cold loved it so[1],
it copied it anew.

Wrapping branches up in ice
Piece by piece it swirled
Like building bricks
Upon these sticks
A gleaming diamond world.

Take a picture with your mind
The crystal world won't last . . .
The warmth will come,
The rising sun
Beginning its work fast.

Crickling-crackling ice becomes
A waterfall below;
The second world
Will melt away
And make the first one grow!

1. With thanks to Lewis Carroll, who wrote in *Alice's Adventures in Wonderland*: "I wonder if the snow loves the trees and fields, that it kisses them so gently? And then it covers them up snug, you know, with a white quilt; and perhaps it says, 'Go to sleep, darlings, till the summer comes again.'"

PONDER..

Frost is made of tiny dewdrops of water that freeze, spreading out little icy arms to touch the little arms of frost next to it, until they've all joined to make a giant, sparkling blanket that wraps around everything in sight, like ice-lace! A bit like this: (*spread out arms and legs, jumping-jack–style, and join hands with each other. See how far you can reach collectively*).

Sometimes, that frost not only spreads out but builds *up* too, like when you stack blocks into a tower. This makes formations of tiny ice crystals—little works of art that can bring a whole lot of beauty, even if we can only see them for a little while before they disappear. But just think: Even though they've disappeared and left all the beauty you can see behind, now they bring invisible beauty by giving life, like making trees grow. Even things that only last a little while can make a difference that lasts forever!

PRAY..

Jesus, frost makes the world look a little bit magical, like a fairy tale. But you're real, better than any fairy tale, and so are the things you do and the things you make! Thank you for giving us a love that's more wonderful than any story we could imagine or make up.

PLAY..

Frost Etch

Find a hard but smooth frost-covered surface, like a window, and let children draw in the frost using the warmth of their fingertips or the scrape of their fingernails. Be careful not to scratch the surface beneath.

If you aren't in a frost-prone area or would prefer to do this activity in the comfort of the indoors, try this version instead.

Materials

- 1 empty tin can, label removed and free of sharp edges
- 1 tablespoon of salt
- Ice

Directions

1. Fill the tin can about halfway with ice.
2. Add the salt.
3. Take turns stirring the ice and salt in the can, or covering the can and shaking it.
4. Watch the layer of frost form on the outside of the can.
5. Invite kids to draw, scribble, or write in the frost using their fingernails.

PAIR...

Prelude and Fugue in C Major, BWV 846
(*The Well-Tempered Clavier*, Book I)

Johann Sebastian Bach

~

Praise the LORD. *How good it is to sing praises to our God,
how pleasant and fitting to praise him! . . .
He spreads the snow like wool and scatters the frost . . .*

PSALM 147:1, 16A NIV

SNOW

Stomp that snow
and
Slosh that slush

Some is aglow
and
Some is mush

The world is a dance
of
echoes and hush

Spin like a snowflake;
There's no rush . . .

PONDER...

Can you feel the way the snow is like a big, soft blanket of quiet?
It paints the world white, spreads it with a hush, and invites us
to pause everything and take joy. The Bible tells us that when we
make mistakes or wrong choices and ask God for forgiveness, He
covers over those things and makes them as white as the snow you
see today (Isaiah 1:18). What a gift!

PRAY ....

Jesus, thank you that you use cold and clouds and water to make
tiny snowflakes, enough to cover everything we can see. The whole
world becomes beautiful, and each tiny snowflake, so different from

the rest, is beautiful too. It reminds us how mighty and strong you are, and how much you care about the small details of our lives!

PLAY

The most magical thing to do with snow is simple, free play. Remember the thrill of diving into a world covered in fluffy white that could be molded and shaped into anything? Tried-and-true favorites are snowmen, snow angels, snowballs, snow forts, snow slides and staircases, snow sculptures, sledding, catching snowflakes in open mouths, or making paper snowflakes inside together.

Bundle up well and have some fun! If you don't have warm snow gear on hand, bring a few big bowls or trays of snow inside and let the kids have fun sculpting it inside until it starts to melt. Offer warm drinks afterward to help warm those brave little hands.

Snow Paint

Mix up a few cups of snow paint using food coloring, water for diluting, and a little cornstarch to thicken just a bit. Kids can use paintbrushes to paint their designs, then lay a "frame" around it using twigs and leaves. Or fill inexpensive squeeze bottles with the paint mixtures and squirt them on the snow to create pictures or designs.

PAIR

Deux Arabesques, L. 66: No. 1 in E Major, Andantino con moto

Claude Debussy

For to the snow he says, "Fall on the earth" ...

JOB 37:6 ESV

ICE

....

(A riddle poem: read poem aloud, then allow kids to guess its title)

Sometimes a ceiling,
Sometimes a floor,
On blades you'll go reeling,
On bobsleds you'll soar

In summer I sing and
I clink in glass walls
In winter I'm king and
Make glass of the world

In the far north
I turn rivers to roads
Add in some warmth
And I make frigid swords

I'm big as a mountain,
Or small as snowflakes
And when I'm around, then
You'll shiver and shake!

Artists can sculpt me
Or build castles too—
You can see through me,
Though sometimes I'm blue!

What am I?

PONDER...

When the world is so cold that water turns to ice, we might really miss some things: the trickle of a stream, the roar of a waterfall, or a favorite lake where you like to play. But even in the middle of missing something, a new thing is happening: God created water to transform into something beautiful that only exists in the cold . . . ice! It makes the world shine, decorates houses with icicles that catch sunlight, and in places like Alaska, it even freezes some rivers solid enough that great big trucks can drive on them like roads! It reminds us that even when things change in our lives, God is always doing something new. We can feel sadness, joy, and anticipation at the same time . . . what a beautiful world!

(Grown-ups, this is a great time to talk about ice safety too: the risk of slipping, the danger of thin ice, etc. Follow all local guidelines for whether/when/how to interact with ice.)

PRAY

Thank you, Lord, that you prepare good things for us in every season of the year, and every season of life. Help us to keep our eyes open with joyful anticipation of what you are creating and doing . . . and thank you for creating us in this time, as part of that beautiful plan!

PLAY

Ice Lanterns

Nest one smaller plastic container (like a bucket) inside of a bigger one and weigh it down with rocks or coins. Fill the space between containers with water and freeze. Once frozen, run cold water over containers until the ice slides easily out; you should have an ice cylinder. On a safe surface (outside on a walkway, inside in glass casserole dish, pie plate, or bowl), place a tea light inside of the ice and light it (discuss candle safety with kids).

Alternately, instead of cylinders, create domed lanterns by filling a few balloons with water. On a flat surface, nestle them to freeze in snow (or in a freezer, surrounded by a kitchen towel "nest" to keep it upright). Once a thick outer layer of ice has formed, remove the balloon "wrapper" from the ice. If you need to flatten the bottom of the dome further, glide it on a warm surface such as a skillet on low. Inside liquid will drain if this is done before it is frozen solid. Light tea light on safe surface and place ice dome over the top . . . enjoy the glow!

Proceed with caution for surfaces and safety, keeping fire danger and water damage in mind as you choose a safe place.

Skate

Find a shallow frozen puddle. Walking kids through some safety pointers, let them twirl and slide! Or visit a local ice rink together in any season to enjoy the magic of ice.

PAIR..

Les Patineurs, Op. 183 ("The Skaters' Waltz")

Émile Waldteufel

⁓

By the breath of God ice is given,
and the broad waters are frozen fast.

JOB 37:10 ESV

Take another look at the poem . . . does its form resemble an igloo?

For more ice fun, search for videos or pictures of ice carousels, ice river roads, ice castles, ice fishing, ice sculptures, blue glacial ice, calving of an iceberg, and igloos.

MORNING

PAUSE

Hush,
The world has slept all night
Dear old world, swim through the light

S t r e t c h,
My arms have slept all night
Come on, arms, swim through the light

Jump,
My legs have slept all night
Ready, legs? Kick through the light!

Light,
Your golden rays are bright
Come, sunlight—Swim through the night!

PONDER

The world feels pretty special in the morning. The light is soft but bright, the air is crisp and new, and the whole day is ahead of you! Did you know that the sunlight you see traveled right past planets in outer space in order to get to you in this moment? Just over eight minutes ago, that sunlight left the sun—and now here it is, on your face and in your hands! If God can make that happen to light your day, just think how He'll be with you, whatever comes. What an adventure!

PLAY ....

Actively Read the Poem

Read the poem again, instructing children to act it out as you read. Lead them in gestures for:

"Hush" (finger to lips, they can whisper the first line with you)

"Stretch . . ." (arms in the air, bending left and right)

"Swim . . ." (act out swimming with arms)

"Jump" (jump in cadence with the poem)

"Kick . . ." (kick)

"Come, sunlight . . ." (gesture a "come here" motion with arm)

PRAY ....

God, just like you light up the world with the sun, your world tells us that we can be a light to the world too (Matthew 5:14). Please fill us with love and joy, and show us chances to be kind to others, to spread that light.

PAIR ....

"Gold und Silber" (Gold and Silver), Op. 79

Franz Lehár

~

This is the day that the LORD has made;
let us rejoice and be glad in it.

PSALM 118:24 ESV

SHADOW

PAUSE..

The sun is painting pictures
in dapples and lines
Casting long shadows
through its steady shine

It reaches out slowly
from way out in space
Unfurling its starlight
and giving slow chase

It runs into objects
the light bounces back!
Collisions of greeting
fall in soft black

"Hello, fine tree branch,
Hello, fine bench
Hello, big building,
Would you like to dance?"

The sun moves around it
in gold somersault
The shadow surrounds it,
a slow-moving waltz

So when I look down,
and my shadow I see . . .
That silvery starlight
is dancing with me!

PONDER ....

Did you know that shadows are made by something blocking the sunlight? It bounces the sunlight back into the air, so it doesn't hit the ground like the rest of the light around it. What's left is called . . . a shadow! As the sun moves throughout the day, shadows change size, shape, and direction. Sometimes, shadows can even go places you can't! You might stand near a wall you can't climb, but guess what? Your shadow can climb right up it! It's a good reminder that God can help us do things we think we can't.

PRAY ....

Lord, shadows tell a beautiful story. They can only exist because of a great, big, beautiful light. And wherever there is a shadow, it means light is on the move! Your Word tells us that you are the light of the world (John 8:12). When your love hits our lives, we pray that others would see how it reaches out and does amazing things.

PLAY ....

Human Sundial

Pick a safe place for your child to stand on the pavement. Using your sidewalk chalk, trace their shadow. Return at different times of day to do the same thing, in the same spot, noticing together the changing sizes and directions of the shadows. Have some fun with silly poses! Write the time of day on each outline, for comparison later. Alternately, you can do the standing, and your child could do the tracing.

PAIR...

"La Précieuse" in the Style of Couperin

Fritz Kreisler

~

Every good and perfect gift is from above,
coming down from the Father of the heavenly lights,
who does not change like shifting shadows.

JAMES 1:17 NIV

SUNSET

PAUSE..

Lift up your eyes at the end of the day
The sky looks alive, and has something to say:

The nighttime is coming, the day is all done
Here is the sunset, where colors are spun

Ribbons of red, and big seas of blue
Pinks into purples, peach, and orange too

The sky seems to whisper, "Please stop for a while . . .
sit back and watch, settle in for a smile."

For what is a sunset? It's clouds and starlight:
Great golden sunrays on seas taking flight

It's faithful like clockwork, each night a display
It's wild in its wonder, it's never the same

So lift up your gaze, it won't come again—
A steal-your-breath sunset's about to begin

PONDER..

There have been many, many sunsets through all of time . . . but never ever one exactly like this one. Tonight's sunset has never happened before and will never happen again in this exact way—and you're here to see it! Isn't it amazing? But perhaps the best part is that a new one will come tomorrow, in an entirely new show of colors and shapes. You might just decide that the sunset is your favorite show!

PRAY ....

Jesus, thank you that you're more faithful than the sunset, and that you care enough about us to create an entirely new display every single night. It reminds us that your mercy is new every day (Lamentations 3:23). Thank you for delighting us and caring for us! Amen.

PLAY ....

Capture the Sunset

Let kids jump and shout out colors as they see them appear. Write them down on the porch, driveway, sidewalk, or street using sidewalk chalk. Watch how your list becomes its own "list poem." Title it "Sunset, [Insert date]" and leave it for others to enjoy. Snap a picture so you can keep the memory! Alternatively, create the list poem on paper for your own family's enjoyment.

PAIR ....

"To a Wild Rose" from *Woodland Sketches*, Op. 51

Edward MacDowell

~

From the rising of the sun to its setting,
the name of the LORD is to be praised!

PSALM 113:3 ESV

NIGHTTIME

PAUSE..

At nighttime the light
Takes on flicker and flight,
In moonlight so gentle,
In fireflies so bright

The air, it grows colder
The stars, they arise
My heart, it grows bolder—
I open my eyes

To see that right here
In the dance of the night
A song fills the earth . . .
Everything is all right.

PONDER..

Take a deep breath. Do you know what's special about that? That's *night air*! When you feel night air filling you up, remember that God made the night, just like He made the day, and it has special stories to tell. Crickets and owls sing, stars shine, and we get to be tucked in safe and warm for the gift of rest.

PRAY ....

God, thank you for making night! Thank you for time to rest and dream, and to know that you are here with us, just like you are during the daytime. Nothing can change that. You make good and beautiful things, and nighttime shows us that too. We ask you tonight for sweet, safe, and peaceful rest.

PLAY ....

Embrace the Night

Lead your child to an open window or even step outside with them if you can. Wrap them in a blanket so they feel cozy and secure next to you. Perhaps even place a cup of warm herbal tea or hot cocoa in their hands for an extra dose of comfort.

Ask, "How do you feel inside that blanket?" (*Warm, cozy, safe, etc.*) "Did you know that God says the darkness is like a blanket over the sea? [Job 38:9 ESV: "I made . . . thick darkness its swaddling band."] At night, lots of the waves grow calm and peaceful because the winds grow calmer too, as the land cools down after the long day. Almost like the waves and wind are getting sleepy! Night air is something special that way. A blanket of calm over creation . . . and that includes us too."

This activity can be done any night but might be especially fitting if a child is having trouble sleeping or is feeling fearful of darkness or night.

PAIR...

Moonlight Sonata: I. Adagio sostenuto

Ludwig van Beethoven

For something lighter:

Nocturne in E Flat Major, H. 24

John Field

~

Yours is the day, yours also the night . . .

PSALM 74:16A ESV

BY THE LIGHT OF THE MOON

PAUSE..

Silver time
Moonlight shines
Deep into the night

Quiet time
Moonlight climbs
Rimming clouds with light

Shadows gentle
Crickets sing
In the dark and bright

Instrumental
Little things
Bringing song to life

Paths unwind:
Friendly, kind,
Bouncing sun's white light

Silver time
Moonlight shines
Treasure in the night

PONDER..

Did you know the moon has no light of its own? It's bouncing the light of the sunlight to us, even when the sun has traveled far across the world. While it's nighttime here, it's daytime there, and the moon borrows some of that daylight to send it to you, right here in the night. God calls it "a faithful witness in the skies" (Psalm 89:37 ESV). A witness is someone who tells the truth, and the moon is always telling us that the sun is shining somewhere, and morning is coming soon.

If God can make a way to do that, He can do anything!

PRAY ....

Thank you, God, for making the moon! It's a reminder to us that daytime is always coming, and that you've made a way for light to be with us, even in the night. We pray that you would bless those who are awake across the world by giving them a wonderful day, and for those who are in the night right now like us, that you would bless them with rest tonight.

PLAY ....

Reflection Detection

Sit next to your child and have them hold a small mirror out in front of them. Play with the mirror at differing angles, letting them see your face in it, reacting to seeing their face in it, even though you're side by side and not looking at each other directly. Have some fun making goofy, surprised, and silly faces.

Ask, "Are you looking at me, or at the mirror?" *(The mirror.)* "But you can still see me! That's just what the moon does for sunlight. Even though we can't see the sun directly right now, we can see its light, thanks to the moon reflecting it to us, like a mirror!"

PAIR..

Clair de Lune, L. 32

Claude Debussy

~

*And God made the two great lights—the greater light to rule the day
and the lesser light to rule the night—and the stars.*

Genesis 1:16 esv

STARGAZING

*

Sun fades
Fading light
Light pricks
Pricking sight

**

Deep dark
Dark night
Night fall
Falls bright

***

Stars come out
Out in space
Spacious sky
Sky embrace

****

PONDER

Have you ever played catch? After the ball leaves your hands, it takes some time for it to travel through the air and reach the place where it lands, right?

Starlight is the same way. When a star releases light, it takes a long time to reach earth. In fact, some stars are *so* far away, it can take hundreds or even thousands of years to get here. Sometimes, that means that the light we're seeing is from a star that has burned out—but its light is still traveling, right to you.

Light from a star that's no longer shining, finding you in this very moment? What a miracle to get to see it!

PRAY

God, your Word says that when we think about the stars, it helps us remember how big you are, how small we are, and most of all, how great your love is for us! (Psalm 8:3–9). Thank you for your great love and power, and for giving us starlight to remember that nothing is impossible for you.

PLAY

Constellation Quest

Spot and name your own constellations. Draw what you see in your nature journal, noting the date. If you repeat this activity over time, notice together how the sky shifts throughout the seasons. Make up stories to go with the shapes you see in the sky—your own family star-lore!

Tip: While summer nights can make for balmy viewing, if you have young kids who are usually asleep before the stars are clear, consider winter nights. Dark falls earlier, and you can bundle up to stay cozy, and warm up with tea or cocoa during your stargazing for some memory-making magic.

PAIR..

Looking Upward: "Beneath the Southern Cross"

John Philip Sousa

~

He determines the number of the stars;
he gives to all of them their names.
Great is our Lord . . .

Psalm 147:4–5a esv

Chain verse *is a poem where the last word of a line is*
also used as the first word of the next line. It makes it feel
a bit like the lines are holding hands . . . Give it a try
together, and have some fun!

JOURNEY'S
END

COMING HOME

PAUSE..

Home is a place to belong:
Four walls, or a heart, or a song
Come in from the journey
And rest all your hurry
Bring pockets of wonder along

We've seen many joys today
Treasures to help light the way
These sights and this story,
These glimpses of glory
Show miracles every day

They tell of a love that came down
Walked on earth, a King without crown
Born to bind up our pains
In great kindness He reigns
As our world spins around and around

Home is God's heart; you belong
He holds you, full of story and song
For wherever you go
Is wherever He'll go
And wherever you are
It is never too far
And wherever you've been
You're now right here with Him . . .

He is loving you here—you belong.

PONDER...

Do you feel tired after our wonder adventure today? It's a good sort of tired—it means we've seen and done a lot, discovered new things, and had fun. God created adventure so that we could explore, learn, have fun, and see how good and mighty He is. What's one thing you saw today that you loved? Let's take some time to thank God for it.

PRAY ....

Dear God, thank you for being our strong tower. Thank you that wherever we go, we have our home right in your heart. Thank you for adventures, and thank you for rest. Thank you for [*insert the things your child listed in the Ponder section*]. You have given us joy today through your creation! We want to bring you joy too. Please fill us up with your love and goodness as we learn and grow.

PLAY ....

Keeping Wonder

Upon returning home, make a special tradition of "processing" whatever treasures you've brought back. Place leaves in your press (or between heavy books, in their own papers or wax paper), or pin them to your wonder garland, or add pebbles, pine cones, shells, twigs, etc. to your growing collection in your wonder jar, or add rocks and twigs to the border of a pathway, flowerbed, or garden in your yard that you're slowly lining with your adventure souvenirs.

Or, coach children in the habit that as soon as they return, they can hang up their jackets, wash their hands, grab their at-home art supplies and/or nature journal, and head to the table or another favorite spot, drawing something they loved from their adventure today while they enjoy a snack.

These traditions can help add a sense of belonging and ownership to the adventures at hand, and they build upon the energy and time investment you've made by allowing reflection, pondering, and creativity. This can also build a sense of anticipation for the next adventure and an air of rest and belonging to the simple act of coming home.

PAIR..

Symphony No. 9, Op. 95: II. Largo (Goin' Home)

Antonín Dvořák (arr. Fischer)

~

The Lord himself goes before you and will be with you;
he will never leave you . . .

Deuteronomy 31:8 NIV

FURTHER RESOURCES

WONDER IN THE WILD

If you venture into landscapes that invite hands-on exploring once your kids are ready to leave the confines of a stroller or wagon, it can sometimes feel daunting. There are so many risks out there—how can we keep kids safe?

While there are many factors that will play into when and whether it's time to seek out places a little wilder, we as caregivers can often find ourselves often uttering two words: "Be careful!"

Whenever possible, take the chance to instead help your child seek out and spot the risks and talk about what being careful actually looks like. This way, rather than repeating "be careful" so often that it risks becoming "invisible" to our children, we're instead equipping them with readiness, caution, courage, and problem-solving.

For example, before entering a wooded area, you might kneel at their level and guide them through looking up, down, all around. Ask questions like, "Do you see anything that could fall? How about anything we could trip on? What animals do you think might live here?" Use a tone of curiosity, to instill awareness rather than fear.

Follow those questions up with, "What are some ways we can take care of those things? How can we make sure we stick together in the forest? How about that creek over there—we know it can be dangerous, but are there safer ways for us to enjoy it?" *(watching from a distance, listening to it, seeing it close up while holding an adult's hand, etc.)*

You'll know what's right for you and the children in your care. Please don't feel a need to venture into a place where the joy of the journey is overshadowed by the risks; there's always a venue fitting your needs in a given season. However, be encouraged that as children grow and are able to think through some of these things with your guidance, your horizons may expand and adventure can be had with care, even when there are variables at play.

INCLEMENT WEATHER WONDER

If you live in an area with seasonally extreme cold or heat keeping you indoors, why not invite nature in?

- Create a "hibernation months" version of your adventure kit, with supplies for observing and interacting with nature inside: salt dough or other ready-made sculpting dough, glue sticks, sketchbooks or journals, magazines for tearing up/cutting up to make collages colored pencils, markers, or other art supplies of your choice. Include any hands-on materials that can add a dose of novelty can help brighten up these months.
- Hang a birdfeeder. Invite kids to sketch what they see, or list observations together, such as colors of birds, what time of day they come, what season they've come in, when you see them more frequently (they require more food when building their nests and gathering food for young). Write a story about one together and give them names. Imagine places in the neighborhood they might

visit today. Provide binoculars or even a small handheld spyglass-style telescope to give an extra flavor of adventure. Play birdsong as white noise in the background. Keep a bird guide on hand for identifying species so you can take the learning and observing deeper.

- Visit wildlife indoors! Spend time at a local animal shelter, animal sanctuary, or nearby stable (make sure to call ahead to see if they are accepting visitors). Or visit a zoo, aquarium, wild animal preserve, or indoor arboretum (many have koi ponds). Bring nature journals to sketch what you see!

- Purchase an ant farm or create one of your own. For the DIY route, find instructions on WonderWoodAdventures.com, where you'll also find tips on how to handle questions about ants that have reached the end of their life cycle. Check out books from the library about ant life to follow along with what they're doing.

- Have a "campout" indoors. Spread sleeping bags on the living room floor, build a blanket fort, or even pitch a tent indoors. Stargaze from the windows or outdoors if weather permits. Make s'mores (supervised) over a candle, in a microwave, or using an indoors s'mores kit. Play games, make shadow puppets, tell stories, read books, have an indoor scavenger hunt, make an extra fun breakfast, and enjoy the memories for years to come!

- Take a deep dive into wilderness and wonder within the pages of picture books. Having noted what captures your child's imagination while out on your adventures, seek out titles containing those topics or creatures. Keep a basket of books handy and reread often to take advantage of the sense of familiarity and ownership that rereading brings. Linger over illustrations together, let kids have "interactive story time" by drawing or painting what they hear, or wherever their imagination takes them. Pull out the sculpting dough and sculpt a creature, scene, or object from the book.

• Start a windowsill herb garden to tend and grow. Use some of the ingredients for a family pizza night, seasoning your sauce or topping the pizza with your homegrown harvest!

CURIOSITY QUESTIONS

It's natural to ask your kids questions to invite them to notice and think. As you do, seek to form questions that are more "curious" than "quiz." Remember, the goal of Curiosity Questions is to *inquire and inspire*, not to drill and quiz.

INSTEAD OF . . .	TRY THIS . . .
What color is that insect?	*What do you notice about that insect?*
(This yields a one-word answer. A fine question for now and then and for some seasons of growth, but a limited experience.)	(This way you can talk about color as well as many other things your kids notice—things we may not have even thought to ask about! The way it walks, its funny antennae, etc. It's open-ended, rather than a one-word answer.)

Curiosity Questions invite pondering, noticing, and further discussion. Encourage kids to ask questions back, to help develop conversational skills. Ask, "What makes you excited about this feather?" Listen to their answers and converse together, then coach: "Would you like to know what I noticed? *You* get to be the one to ask the curiosity question! Just say, 'What makes you excited about it?'" As time goes on, they'll know how to do this and will need less coaching.

Some Curiosity Question starters:

• What do you notice about . . . ?
• What makes you excited about . . . ?

- How do you think this happened? (nest, sand formation, etc.)
- What do you think that [creature's name] will do today?
- What do you think it would feel like to . . . ?

WONDERING WHETHER

There are times when it's tempting to think of wonder outings as trivial in light of especially difficult current events, whether worldwide or on a more personal/family level. On those days, if you're wondering whether to embark and whether doing so is disrespectful or trivial, may I offer a gentle invitation to go ahead and venture into that wonder-realm anyway?

It will likely prove to be exactly the opposite of your worries. Instead of trivializing anything, being in God's creation can help bring perspective, comfort, and hope. Your decision to do something to help sow those things is a quiet but courageous act of defiance against darkness. Journey forth, and do that good work, even in the hard moments.

But do so with a spirit of grace, remembering that on this journey of wonder, there are no expectations or requirements. Skip the poem and activities if you'd like, if the jovial tone doesn't suit the day. But step outside and you may just find that there is comfort in seeing the now-familiar fingerprints of God's handiwork, the truths we've explored within this book: that He is here. He is mighty. He is gentle. He is close to the brokenhearted. And He is present in your hour of need. He is pouring forth evidence upon evidence that He holds your heart so close, and the hearts of your little ones too. If you're "wondering whether," this may be the exact right time to do so. An act of hope, just when it's needed. Sometimes wonder looks like delight . . . but other times, it looks like comfort, right where it feels impossible.

Thou art worthy, O Lord, to receive glory and honour and power: for thou hast created all things, and for thy pleasure they are and were created.

Revelation 4:11 KJV

FIELD NOTES

A PLACE TO RECORD QUOTES, MEMORIES, OUTINGS

AMANDA DYKES is the winner of the prestigious 2020 Christy Award Book of the Year, a *Booklist* 2019 Top Ten Romance debut, and the winner of an INSPY award for her debut novel *Whose Waves These Are* as well as her other novels, including *Set the Stars Alight*, the book that first awoke her spirit to God's gift of wonder as a means of fighting darkness and mining for hope. A former English teacher, Amanda is a drinker of tea, dweller of redemption, and spinner of hope-filled tales who spends most days chasing wonder and words with her family. Find her online at AmandaDykes.com.